LJ

D0478493

AUG 31 2012

THE AMEN SOLUTION

EAT HEALTHY

with THE BRAIN DOCTOR'S *Wife*

Cookbook

3 1336 09003 2799

SAN DIEGO PUBLIC
LIBRARY
LA JOLLA

TANA AMEN, B.S.N.
with Kamila Reschke

Copyright 2011 by MindWorks Press

All rights reserved. No part of this program may be reproduced or transmitted in any form or by any means, electronic or mechanical, including photocopying without the written permission of the publisher.

Published by MindWorks Press, Newport Beach, California.

A Division of Amen Clinics, Inc.

www.amenclinics.com

Authors: Tana Amen, BSN & Kamila Reschke

Photographer: Jim Kennedy

Layout and Design: Jaclyn Frattali

Cover Art: Rick Cortez

Printed in China

OTHER BOOKS BY TANA AMEN

GET HEALTHY WITH THE BRAIN DOCTOR'S WIFE COACHING GUIDE, MindWorks Press, 2011

CHANGE YOUR BRAIN, CHANGE YOUR BODY COOKBOOK, MindWorks Press, 2010

Dedication:

To my mother and grandmother for nurturing my culinary talents.
Love, Kamila

-and-

To my mother, Mary for always being an example of strength and perseverance.
I love you mom! - Tana

Table of Contents

Daniel G. Amen, M.D.

It seemed that many women in our neighborhood referred to my wife Tana as "the brain doctor's wife." After hearing this over and over, I knew that should be the title for her new series of books: *Eat Healthy With The Brain Doctor's Wife: A Cookbook* and *Get Healthy With The Brain Doctor's Wife: A Coaching Guide.*

Tana is constantly being asked for health and nutrition tips in the neighborhood, at school, nearly everywhere she goes. And, when people actually do what she suggests they get dramatically positive health benefits. The phone calls and emails she gets about people losing abdominal pain, improving their energy, losing weight, and even having regular bowel movements never cease to amaze us because it is all so easy. Both of us advocate: eat high quality foods and avoid foods that are poisoning you. It sounds simple, but our society is not helping us. Nearly everywhere we go we are being bombarded by the wrong messages that are making us fat, depressed, and feebleminded.

Tana has a passion for health. When we met she was a neurosurgical intensive care nurse and worked with very sick patients who had severe brain problems. Through our joint efforts she has worked hard to help people get and stay healthy, so they could avoid the hospital and the illnesses that predisposed people to strokes, heart disease, diabetes, and Alzheimer's disease.

The principles in this series are the same as those I discuss in *The Amen Solution: Brain Healthy Ways to Lose Weight and Keep It Off*. Here is a brief summary:

Food is your best medicine or it can be your worst enemy. The typical Western diet of bad fat, salt, and sugar (think cheeseburgers, fries, and sodas) promotes inflammation and has been associated by itself with depression, ADD, dementia, heart disease, cancer, diabetes, and obesity.

But if you start making better choices today, you will quickly notice that you have more energy, better focus, better memory, better moods, and a slimmer, sexier waistline.

A number of new studies have reported that a healthy diet is associated with dramatically lower risks of Alzheimer's disease and depression.

Plus, what really surprised me when I decided to get healthy was my food choices got better not worse. It was the start of a wonderful relationship with food, rather than being a slave to foods that were hurting me. I used to be like a yo-yo: crave bad food, overeat it, feel lousy, then hate myself in the process.

It was way too much drama. Since I have been on our program, I have never eaten better and it affects everything in my life in a positive way. I don't want fast food anymore, because it makes me tired and stupid. I want the right food that makes me smarter. And, contrary to what most people think, eating in a brain healthy way is not more expensive; it is less expensive. My medical bills are lower and my productivity has gone way up. And what price can you put on feeling amazing? Why not be smart and use food as medicine that heals you?

To help you navigate your way to the best options that will help you slim down, boost your cognitive function, and lift your mood, we have come up with the following rules to eat by.

Amen Clinics 7 Rules for Brain Healthy Eating

Rule #1 Think high-quality calories in and high-quality energy out.
To lose weight, you have to count calories. Not counting your calories is like not knowing how much money you have in the bank, and yet you continue to spend, spend, spend and wonder why you're bankrupt. It is not as simple as calories in versus calories out. Focus on eating high-quality calories. A 250-calorie candy bar is not the same thing as a bowl of lentil soup, a piece of wild salmon, or a walnut and blueberry salad. "High-quality energy out" means you need to rev

your metabolism in healthy ways. Exercise, new learning, and green tea help. Diet pills, sugary caffeinated energy drinks, excessive coffee, caffeinated sodas, and smoking are low-quality energy boosters.

Rule #2 Drink plenty of water and not too many of your calories.
Your brain is 80 percent water. Anything that dehydrates it, such as too much caffeine or alcohol, decreases your thinking and impairs your judgment. On a trip to New York City, I saw a poster that read, "Are You Pouring On The Pounds... Don't Drink Yourself Fat." I thought it was brilliant. A recent study found that on average Americans drink 450 calories a day, twice as many as we did 30 years ago. Just adding an extra 225 calories a day will put 23 pounds of fat on your body a year, and most people tend to not count the calories they drink.

Rule #3 Eat high-quality lean protein throughout the day.

Protein helps balance your blood sugar, boosts concentration, and provides the necessary building blocks for brain health. Great sources of protein include fish, skinless turkey or chicken, beans, raw nuts, low-fat or non-fat dairy, and high-protein vegetables, such as broccoli and spinach.

Rule #4 Eat low-glycemic, high-fiber carbohydrates.

This means eat carbohydrates that do not spike your blood sugar and that are also high in fiber, such as those found in vegetables, fruits, beans, and whole grains. Carbohydrates are NOT the enemy. They are essential to your life. Bad carbohydrates are the enemy. These are carbohydrates that have been robbed of any nutritional value, such as simple sugars and refined carbohydrates. Sugar is not your friend. Sugar increases inflammation in your body, increases erratic brain-cell firing, and has been recently implicated in aggression. The less sugar in your life, the better your life will be.

Rule #5 Focus your diet on healthy fats.

Eliminate bad fats, such as ALL trans-fats and most animal fat. Did you know that fat stores toxic materials? So when you eat animal fat, you are also eating anything toxic the animal ate. Yuck. Did you know that certain fats that are found in pizza, ice cream, and cheeseburgers fool the brain into ignoring the signals that you should be full? No wonder it's so hard to stop at just one slice of pizza! Focus your diet on healthy fats, especially those that contain omega-3 fatty acids, found in foods like salmon, avocados, walnuts, and green leafy vegetables.

Rule #6 Eat from the rainbow.

This means put natural foods in your diet of many different colors, such as blueberries, pomegranates, yellow squash, and red bell peppers. This will boost the antioxidant levels in your body and help keep your brain young. Of course, this does not mean Skittles or jelly beans.

Rule #7 Cook with brain healthy herbs & spices to boost your brain and lose your belly.

Trading in heavy cream sauces for herbs and spices can help you trim calories. Here are other ways herbs and spices help:

- Turmeric, found in curry, contains a chemical that has been shown to decrease the plaques in the brain thought to be responsible for Alzheimer's disease.

- In four studies, a saffron extract was found to be as effective as antidepressant medication in treating people with major depression.

- There is very good scientific evidence that Sage helps to boost memory.

- Cinnamon has been shown to help attention and regulate blood sugar levels. Research also shows that cinnamon extract can inhibit the tau aggregation associated with Alzheimer's disease.

Be smart with your food and you will be smarter overall!

Tana takes these principles and helps you incorporate them into your life in a very practical way. She gives you hundreds of tips and suggestions to get started immediately to develop brain healthy food habits. Plus, Tana and our wonderful cook Kamila Reschke give you great, tasty, easy-to-prepare recipes to make brain healthy eating easy and satisfying.

I feel eternally blessed to have Tana as my life partner and Kamila as a trusted friend. I know you too will feel blessed to have met them to help you on your path to get thinner, smarter, and happier.

To your brain health,

Daniel G. Amen, MD

Medical Director and CEO, Amen Clinics, Inc.

Getting Started
Chapter 1

By now many of you know that health and fitness are a way of life in the Amen household. What you probably don't know is that I don't actually like cooking, which is funny for someone who is writing her second cookbook. And I absolutely hate anything that even sounds like or resembles a diet! But I am passionate about continuing education and teaching. And in order to feed my family healthy, nutritious fare and avoid the toxic garbage that is so often passed off as food in our society, I did have to learn the basics of cooking. As a result, I was determined to get this "cooking thing" down to a science with simple, nu-

tritious meals that are a balance of high-quality proteins, healthy essential fats, and complex carbohydrates (mostly in the form of vegetables and fruits).

The food you eat can either be your best medicine, or a drug that will take you on a really bad trip! The Amen Solution emphasizes foods that optimize brain function, decrease systemic inflammation, increase satiety, break the chain of food addictions by balancing the hormones of hunger and satiety, offer high-quality calories, and provide greater quantities of micronutrients even though they are calorie-sparse (think "more bang for your buck"). It also focuses on a lifestyle of eating that will have you feeling energized and satisfied instead of deprived.

With our cook Kamila helping to design recipes, nutrition has taken on a whole new dimension. I am constantly challenging Kamila's culinary skills. Strictly adhering to my nutrition principles, she often has her hands full trying to come up with alternatives to classic recipes that will pass the taste test for the rest of the family. Although she often mutters under her breath and gives me the "evil eye," she never lets me down. She always delivers incredibly healthy alternatives to any recipe I give her and has

come up with dozens of her own. We are very excited to share our principles and our recipes for health with you in this new cookbook.

If it were up to me, it would be very simple. I would have you all eating a diet closely resembling that of a gorilla! Massive amounts of veggies, a little fruit, nuts, and seeds... and maybe a little more animal protein than gorillas eat (since we don't have all day to sit around eating leaves). That's not far off from how I eat, and how we have designed many of these recipes. But realizing that one nutritional plan does not fit all, we have tried to give you a lot of options to fit your individual needs and tastes.

People often ask me why the ingredients in my cookbooks aren't all "mainstream" items they can buy in any grocery store. Why can't you just use the same old stuff you are familiar with? Well, in case you haven't noticed... that's the problem! The definition of insanity is continuing to do the same thing and expecting a different outcome. We have tried to use as many "mainstream" ingredients as possible. However, the main purpose of this book is to help you change the way you view health, nutrition, and food. We want to break your old food addictions and unhealthy habits. That requires some tweaking of the ingredients you have been using. This way of cooking may seem unfamiliar to you at first, but if you give us 30 days, you will come to love these new ingredients. If you give us 12 weeks, you will never turn back!

Tana's "Not So Humble" Opinion

Besides being a nurse and having a background in science and fitness, I have learned a lot about health and nutrition through trial, error, and a tremendous amount of research. I have some very strong opinions about optimal nutrition, but I understand that one nutritional plan does not fit all people. That is why this cookbook offers a wide variety of recipes, including vegan, vegetarian, gluten-free, and grain-free recipes. In many of the recipes, you will find helpful notes on how to modify the recipes to suit your particular plan.

My personal preference for general health, and especially for anyone trying to lose weight, is to avoid all bread, flour, grains, and dairy for at least the first two weeks. I believe everyone should be tested for hidden food sensitivities, especially to gluten, other grains, and lectins. Lectins are sugar-binding proteins that act as a natural "pesticide" in most plants and foods that we eat. They are not easily broken down and processed by the human body, and they bind to the intestinal lining, causing irritation and damage... not to mention leptin resistance and, eventually, insulin resistance as they do so (more for some people than for others). They are more highly concentrated in some foods than others, and more irritating if foods are not prepared properly. Eating a diet high in grains, dairy, and legumes can wreak havoc on your weight-loss plan and your general health if you have undiscovered sensitivities to these little buggers (as I did), and/or if you do not prepare these foods correctly when you do consume them. Legumes and grains need to be soaked and fully cooked before consuming them.

Additionally, the more breads, grains, and starchy carbs you consume, the more sugar and carbs you will crave... and the hungrier you will be. The less of them you eat, the more satisfied you will be! There is a reason to ditch them for at least the first few weeks. You will find some recipes containing whole grains and legumes in this cookbook, but we highly recommend that you focus on these treats as "condiments" and eat them sparingly.

My favorite "meals" are the smoothies, salads, soups, fish, and grain-free dishes... and there are lots of them within these pages! I hope you will find a lot of new favorites, too!

Good luck and bon appétit!

Brain Healthy Spices

Organize your spice cabinet with the list of brain healthy spices discussed in detail in *The Amen Solution*. I use a lot of these spices in the recipes. Although I prefer to cook with fresh herbs when possible, I recommend that you also have dried herbs available for convenience and saving time. Here are some of my favorites for brain health:

- **Saffron**: improves memory and helps to support positive mood.

- **Curry**: potent antioxidant, anti-inflammatory agent and helps to decrease the plaques thought to be responsible for Alzheimer's disease.

- **Oregano**: potent antioxidant and may help with PMS and insomnia.

- **Basil**: potent antioxidant, improves blood flow to the brain and may help memory.

- **Cinnamon**: improves working memory and ability to pay attention.

- **Garlic**: improves blood flow to the brain and increases immunity.

- **Ginger**: potent anti-aging and anti-inflammatory properties.

- **Thyme**: increases DHA (an important fat) in the brain.

- **Sage**: improves memory and overall mental functioning.

- **Rosemary**: antioxidant and has anti-inflammatory properties.

- **Marjoram:** promotes healthy digestion and can soothe minor digestive upsets.

- **Sea Salt:** that has not been bleached and chemically altered.

Go Easy with the "Spice of Life"

Please note that we do not have salt measurements on most of our recipes by design. Added salt is not accounted for in the nutritional charts. If you ask for a nutritional chart in most restaurants, you will be astounded at the amount of sodium used in soups and other low-fat items. If you want to regain control of your metabolism and taste buds, which have been hijacked by the excessive amounts of fat, salt, and sugar in the American diet, you need to start by cutting back on salt, as well as the other ingredients listed, and being aware of how much you use. If you are overweight there is a good chance you also have an issue with high blood pressure. Using a lot of salt is literally "adding salt to the wound" when it comes to high blood pressure. Since most people add salt to their food anyway, we do not cook with much salt nor do we automatically add it to recipes. When using salt, we recommend using unbleached salts, such as pink Himalayan sea salt or some other salt that has not had the minerals removed... and we suggest using it lightly.

Get Familiar with the "Brain Health Basic Ingredients"

As you get cooking, you will notice that some ingredients pop up in many of the recipes. That is because they are some of the healthiest choices for your brain and body. Most of the ingredients are basic and can be found in any grocery store, but a few of them may be new to you and might be easier to find at your local health food store. You can also try ordering them online. I have found that I can often save a bundle this way.

Stock up on these "Brain Health Must-Have Ingredients":

- **Coconut oil**
- **Almond oil**
- **Cacao powder**
- **Cacao nibs**
- **Liquid stevia sweetener (various flavors)**
- **Goji berries**
- **Raw, shaved coconut**
- **Almond milk, unsweetened**

- **Vegan protein powder, sugar free (sweetened with stevia): I like Olympian Labs Pea Protein or Tony Gonzalez (All-Pro Science®) brands**
- **Flax seeds**
- **Chia seeds**
- **Raw, unsalted nuts**
- **Hemp seeds and hemp seed oil**

- **Freeze-dried greens: Green Vibrance® is a great brand**
- **Quinoa**
- **Vegenaise®**
- **Earth Balance® (butter replacement)**
- **Tamari sauce**
- **Soy or nut cheese**
- **Arrowroot**

- **Soy creamer:** I am not a huge fan of soy products when used in excess. For example, drinking soy milk by the glass can be troublesome because it takes a whole lot of soybeans to make a single glass of soy milk. A few soybeans (organic), however, are fine and actually have some health benefits. That is why we use a little soy creamer in some of the recipes for thickening.

- **Shirataki noodles:** I like the brand called "Miracle Noodles®." This is by far one of my best discoveries for a healthy alternative to pasta. They are virtually calorie-free, fat-free and low-carb, containing only three grams of carbs for an entire package. The carbs they do contain are soluble fiber, which slows digestion and allows for slower absorption of sugar. That means they keep you feeling full longer and don't cause your blood sugar to spike. Shirataki noodles are made from the root of the konnyaku imo plant (a yam-like vegetable). They are inexpensive and can be purchased in bulk online or at Whole Foods®. They have a slightly different consistency than regular pasta, so I wouldn't suggest eating them plain. But if you add a nutritious sauce, they are great!

Get Smart About Cooking Oils

Although olive oil and many other oils are very nutritious when consumed on salads or in "raw" form, they are toxic when heated to high temperatures. For cooking we usually use coconut oil or grape seed oil. Although I am not an advocate of dairy, when cooking at high temperatures, I do advocate raw, organic butter or ghee (depending on the use). When oils reach their smoking point during cooking, they become toxic. Coconut oil and grape seed oil have a higher smoking point than olive oil, as does butter. I still prefer coconut oil over butter, but at times the flavor of coconut oil might interfere with what you are preparing.

Most of the recipes in this book suggest using vegetable broth for sautéing instead of oil. In most cases you don't even need oil for cooking vegetables. When using oil, use it sparingly.

{ Learn to Use Healthy Alternatives }

It is far easier to replace a habit than to eliminate it. A few examples:

→ Replace pasta with Shirataki noodles! I order "Miracle Noodles®" online.

→ Replace bleached salt with unbleached sea salt.

→ Replace dairy with almond milk, hemp milk or rice milk.

→ Replace sugar with stevia. When you must use a real sweetener try to use raw, unfiltered honey or pure maple syrup, and use a fraction of the amount.

→ Replace commercial cocoa with raw, unsweetened cacao.

→ Replace chocolate chips with raw cacao nibs or unsweetened carob chips. You still need to watch the quantity if you use carob, but they contain half the amount of fat and sugar as chocolate.

→ Replace ice cream with "Avocado Gelato" (see page 197).

→ Replace candy with sugar-free "Brain On Joy" bars. These can be found on the website www.amenclinics.com.

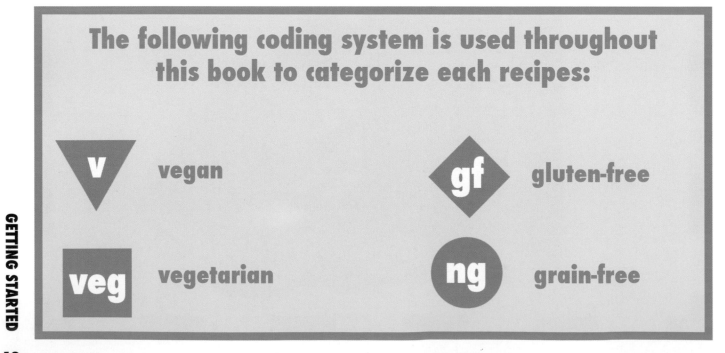

The following coding system is used throughout this book to categorize each recipes:

v vegan

gf gluten-free

veg vegetarian

ng grain-free

Tana's Tips for Success

1. **Purchase fresh, organic produce when possible.** The pesticide residual from non-organic produce is more concentrated in some fruits and vegetables than others, leading to many brain and health issues. When you can't get fresh organic produce, choose organic frozen fruits and vegetables over canned.

2. **Clean out your pantry and make room for the wonderful new additions you will be purchasing.** Make one decision (not to have it in your house) instead of 30 decisions (to stay away from it if it is in your pantry.)

3. **When preparing foods, always prepare enough to have leftovers for the next day.**

4. **Stay hydrated! Drink half your body weight in ounces.** If you weigh 180 pounds, drink 90 ounces of water. If it's hard to drink that much plain water, try flavoring it with a little lemon and some lemon-flavored liquid stevia. Stevia is a natural sugar substitute that does not affect blood sugar levels.

5. **Know your suggested daily protein intake.** The average daily protein intake of a healthy individual should be approximately 0.8 grams of protein per kilogram of ideal body weight. A kilogram is 2.2 pounds. Figure out your weight in kilograms (your weight in pounds divided by 2.2). Then multiply your weight in kilograms by 0.8. Divide this number equally by the number of meals that you eat throughout the day to determine how much protein you should eat with each meal (this doesn't need to include snacks)... and remember this is an estimate. It's not a big deal if you go a little over or a little under. For example: I weigh 124 pounds. I divide 124 by 2.2, which is 56.4. Multiply that by 0.8. The average amount of protein I should consume on a daily basis is about 46 grams per day. I divide that by 3, and make sure I consume at least 15 grams of protein with each meal. Since I often work out very intensely, I don't worry about getting a little extra protein. I eat so many greens and nuts, that my average protein intake is more likely around 20 grams per meal. I am very conscious to drink lots of water for kidney health.

Brain-Boosting Smoothies

Chapter 2

Our Favorite Way to Start the Day: Chapter 2

Smoothies are one of my favorite ways to optimize nutrition and treat my family and myself to a tasty, refreshing raw meal loaded with water-rich phytonutrients, vitamins, minerals, and fiber.

Some Basics About Additives:

→ If the raw greens are too much initially, start slow and gradually increase the amount you add. Sometimes it's an acquired taste.

→ You may need to add a teaspoon of raw honey or agave in the beginning, but try to wean away from it as soon as possible. If it works to get your kids eating their veggies, use it, then gradually decrease the amount.

→ Raw cacao is the pure form of cocoa before it has been processed. It is loaded with antioxidants and phytonutrients. It is one of my favorite additives for smoothies. It can be found in most health food stores.

→ Cacao nibs are cacao beans that have been coarsely ground. They are great for adding a chocolate chip texture to desserts and smoothies. Kids usually love them and they are sugar free!

→ Pure coconut water is God's natural "sports drink." It is loaded with electrolytes, and has a lot less sugar and other chemicals than most sports drinks.

→ I love adding fiber to my smoothies for that extra boost.

→ Things like bee pollen, aloe gel, maca root, goji powder and other "super foods" can be excellent additives. Many of these super foods are known antioxidants or have anti-inflammatory properties, but these claims have not all been clinically proven. As with all ingredients, pay attention to calories and fat content.

Benefits of Brain-Boosting Smoothies:

Delicious, simple, quick...
nutrition on the run!

Children love them

You can "hide" many nutritious additives
(like greens) without them being detected

**Water-rich, loaded with vitamins,
minerals, fiber and phytonutrients**

Very satisfying

**You can custom design them to fit your
taste and nutritional needs**

BRAIN-BOOSTING SMOOTHIES

Very Omega Cherry

Makes 2 Servings

Ingredients:

1 cup organic cherries, frozen

8 ounces almond milk, unsweetened

1 cup baby spinach (I promise you can't taste it, but you can adjust the amount initially until you get used to it if necessary.)

2-3 kale leaves (work with me... just try it!)

¼ cup raw pecans (or other nuts)

1 tablespoon chia seeds

1 scoop sugar-free vanilla protein powder (I prefer pea or rice protein sweetened with stevia. Use 2 scoops for large men.)

1 tablespoon freeze-dried greens (Green Vibrance® is one of my favorite brands.)

1 dropper full vanilla crème-flavored liquid stevia

Optional Additives:

Fiber

Bee Pollen

Aloe Gel

Preparation:

1. Add all ingredients to blender bowl.

2. Turn blender on low at first, then increase speed.

3. Add additional water or almond milk as needed to achieve desired consistency.

4. Pour into glasses and serve cold.

Nutritional information per serving:

281 calories	129 mg sodium
16 g fat	29 g carbohydrates
1 g saturated fat	9 g fiber
0 mg cholesterol	14 g protein

BRAIN-BOOSTING SMOOTHIES

Berry Alert

gf   ng   v

Ingredients:

1 cup organic blueberries, frozen

8 ounces pure coconut water or almond milk, unsweetened

1 large handful baby spinach – about 1½ cups (I promise you can't taste it, but you can adjust the amount initially until you get used to it if necessary.)

¼ avocado (about 2 tablespoons)

2 tablespoons flax seeds

1 scoop sugar-free vanilla or berry protein powder (I prefer pea or rice protein sweetened with stevia. Use 2 scoops for large men.)

1 tablespoon freeze-dried greens (Green Vibrance® is one of my favorite brands.)

1 dropper full vanilla crème-flavored liquid stevia

Optional Additives:

Fiber

Bee Pollen

Aloe Gel

Preparation:

1. Add all ingredients to blender bowl.

2. Turn blender on low at first, then increase speed.

3. Add additional water or coconut water as needed to achieve desired consistency.

4. Pour into glasses and serve cold.

Nutritional information per serving:

230 calories	69 mg sodium
9 g fat	32 g carbohydrates
1 g saturated fat	9 g fiber
0 mg cholesterol	14 g protein

v ng gf

Ingredients:

½ pink grapefruit, peeled

1 large orange, peeled

1 carrot, unpeeled

1 cup iceberg lettuce

1 tablespoon hemp seeds

1 tablespoon raw sunflower seeds

1 scoop sugar-free vanilla protein powder (I prefer pea or rice protein sweetened with stevia. Use 2 scoops for large men.)

1 tablespoon freeze-dried greens (Green Vibrance® is one of my favorite brands.)

1 dropper full orange-flavored liquid stevia

Handful of ice cubes

Optional Additives:

Fiber

Bee Pollen

Aloe Gel

Preparation:

1. Add all ingredients to blender bowl.

2. Turn blender on low at first, then increase speed.

3. Add additional water or almond milk as needed to achieve desired consistency.

4. Pour into glasses and serve cold.

Nutritional information per serving:

228 calories	62 mg sodium
7 g fat	32 g carbohydrates
1 g saturated fat	7 g fiber
0 mg cholesterol	15 g protein

BRAIN-BOOSTING SMOOTHIES

v   **ng**   **gf**

Ingredients:

1 large organic apple

1 organic carrot, unpeeled

8 ounces pure coconut water or almond milk, unsweetened

1 cup baby spinach or chard (I promise you can't taste it, but you can adjust the amount initially until you get used to it if necessary.)

½ organic cucumber, unpeeled

¼ cup raw walnuts (or other nuts)

1 tablespoon flax seeds

1 scoop sugar-free vanilla protein powder (I prefer pea or rice protein sweetened with stevia. Use 2 scoops for large men.)

1 tablespoon freeze-dried greens (Green Vibrance® is one of my favorite brands.)

1 dropper full vanilla crème-flavored liquid stevia

Handful of ice cubes

Optional Additives:

Fiber

Bee Pollen

Aloe Gel

Preparation:

1. Add all ingredients to blender bowl.

2. Turn blender on low at first, then increase speed.

3. Add additional water or almond milk as needed to achieve desired consistency.

4. Pour into glasses and serve cold.

Nutritional information per serving:

300 calories	71 mg sodium
15 g fat	35 g carbohydrates
2 g saturated fat	10 g fiber
0 mg cholesterol	15 g protein

BRAIN-BOOSTING SMOOTHIES

Chocolate-Kissed Sunset

gf ng v

Ingredients:

1 large orange, peeled

½ green apple

1 tablespoon dried goji berries

8 ounces pure coconut water

1 cup baby spinach

¼ cup pecans

1 tablespoon Chia seeds (or flax seeds)

1 scoop sugar-free chocolate protein powder (I prefer pea or rice protein sweetened with stevia. Use 2 scoops for large men.)

1 tablespoon freeze-dried greens (Green Vibrance® is one of my favorite brands.)

1 dropper full chocolate- or orange-flavored liquid stevia

Handful of ice cubes

Optional: 1 teaspoon raw cacao, unsweetened (found in health food stores)

Optional: 1 tablespoon raw coconut, shaved and unsweetened

Preparation:

1. Add all ingredients to blender bowl.

2. Turn blender on low at first, then increase speed.

3. Add additional water or almond milk as needed to achieve desired consistency.

4. Pour into glasses and serve cold.

Optional Additives:

Fiber

Bee Pollen

Aloe Gel

Nutritional information per serving:

311 calories	92 mg sodium
15 g fat	42 g carbohydrates
1 g saturated fat	10 g fiber
0 mg cholesterol	15 g protein

Chunky Chocolate Monkey

v   ng   gf

This is a favorite with children and a great way to introduce them to greens and raw food. Start out using only avocado, as your children get used to drinking smoothies try adding a small amount of spinach. They will likely never notice.

Ingredients:

1 slightly green banana

¼ avocado (about 2 tablespoons)

8 ounces almond milk, unsweetened

¼ cup raw macadamia nuts or almonds

1 tablespoon raw coconut, unsweetened and shaved

1 scoop sugar-free chocolate protein powder (I prefer pea or rice protein sweetened with stevia. Use 2 scoops for large men.)

1 tablespoon freeze-dried greens (Green Vibrance® is one of my favorite brands.)

1-2 teaspoons raw cacao, unsweetened (found in health food stores)

1 dropper full chocolate-flavored liquid stevia

Handful of ice cubes

Optional: 1 tablespoon raw cacao nibs, unsweetened (they taste like chocolate chips)

Optional Additives:

Fiber

Bee Pollen

Aloe Gel

Preparation:

1. Add all ingredients to blender bowl.

2. Turn blender on low at first, then increase speed.

3. Add additional water or almond milk as needed to achieve desired consistency.

4. Pour into glasses and serve cold.

Nutritional information per serving:

283 calories	113 mg sodium
14 g fat	32 g carbohydrates
2 g saturated fat	8 g fiber
0 mg cholesterol	14 g protein

BRAIN-BOOSTING SMOOTHIES

Tropical Storm

gf ng v

Take a sip of this refreshing smoothie, and you'll feel like you're on a sandy beach in the South Pacific. Tropical coconut is so good for you and it is considered to be a "functional food," meaning it has health benefits beyond its nutritional offerings.

Ingredients:

½ cup pineapple, cubed

1 slightly green banana

8 ounces pure coconut water

1 cup iceberg lettuce

½ organic cucumber, unpeeled

¼ cup raw macadamia nuts (or other nuts)

2 tablespoons raw coconut, shaved

1 tablespoon flax seeds

1 scoop sugar-free vanilla protein powder (I prefer pea or rice protein sweetened with stevia. Use 2 scoops for large men.)

1 tablespoon freeze-dried greens (Green Vibrance® is one of my favorite brands.)

1 dropper full vanilla crème- or orange-flavored liquid stevia

Handful of ice cubes

Optional Additives:

Fiber

Bee Pollen

Aloe Gel

Preparation:

1. Add all ingredients to blender bowl.

2. Turn blender on low at first, then increase speed.

3. Add additional water or almond milk as needed to achieve desired consistency.

4. Pour into glasses and serve cold

Nutritional information per serving:

357 calories	54 mg sodium
19 g fat	43 g carbohydrates
4 g saturated fat	9 g fiber
0 mg cholesterol	14 g protein

Coco Mint Madness

Makes 2 Servings

gf ng v

Ingredients:

2 tablespoons raw coconut, unsweetened and shaved (or the meat of one coconut)

½ slightly green banana

½ apple

2 tablespoons raw macadamia nuts or almonds

8 ounces pure coconut water, unsweetened

4-5 fresh mint leaves

1 cup iceberg lettuce or spinach

1 scoop sugar-free chocolate protein powder (I prefer pea or rice protein sweetened with stevia. Use 2 scoops for large men.)

1 tablespoon freeze-dried greens (Green Vibrance® is one of my favorite brands.)

1 teaspoon raw cacao, unsweetened (found in health food stores)

1 dropper full chocolate-flavored liquid stevia

Handful of ice cubes

Optional: 1 tablespoon raw cacao nibs, unsweetened (they taste like chocolate chips)

Optional Additives:

Fiber

Bee Pollen

Aloe Gel

Preparation:

1. Add all ingredients to blender bowl.

2. Turn blender on low at first, then increase speed.

3. Add additional water or almond milk as desired to achieve desired consistency.

4. Pour into glasses and serve cold.

Nutritional information per serving:

175 calories	50 mg sodium
4 g fat	31 g carbohydrates
2 g saturated fat	5 g fiber
0 mg cholesterol	11 g protein

Everything But the Kitchen Sink- V-7 Cleanse

v ng gf

Ingredients: (all organic vegetables)

1 small tomato

½ red bell pepper

1 carrot, unpeeled

½ cucumber, unpeeled

1 cup spinach

½ avocado

1 teaspoon fresh ginger

10-12 ounces cold water

2 tablespoons flax seeds

1 tablespoon freeze-dried greens (Green Vibrance® is one of my favorite brands.)

Handful of ice

Optional: 1 scoop sugar-free unflavored protein powder (I prefer pea or rice protein sweetened with stevia. Use 2 scoops for large men.)

** Consider flavoring with a few drops of tamari or Tabasco® sauce.

Optional Additives:

Fiber

Bee Pollen

Aloe Gel

Preparation:

1. Add all ingredients to blender bowl.

2. Turn blender on low at first, then increase speed.

3. Add additional water or almond milk as desired to achieve desired consistency.

4. Pour into glasses and serve cold

Nutritional information per serving:

198 calories	59 mg sodium
12 g fat	20 g carbohydrates
1 g saturated fat	10 g fiber
0 mg cholesterol	6 g protein

Chocolate Covered Strawberry

v ng gf

Ingredients:

1 cup organic strawberries, frozen

¼ avocado (about 2 tablespoons)

8 ounces unsweetened almond milk

1 cup baby spinach

1 tablespoon sunflower seeds

1 scoop sugar-free chocolate protein powder (I prefer pea or rice protein sweetened with stevia. Use 2 scoops for large men.)

1 tablespoon freeze-dried greens (Green Vibrance© is one of my favorite brands.)

1 dropper full chocolate-flavored liquid stevia

Optional: 1 teaspoon raw cacao, unsweetened (found in health food stores)

Optional Additives:

Fiber

Bee Pollen

Aloe Gel

Preparation:

1. Add all ingredients to blender bowl.

2. Turn blender on low at first, then increase speed.

3. Add additional water or almond milk as desired to achieve desired consistency.

4. Pour into glasses and serve cold

Nutritional information per serving:

201 calories	124 mg sodium
9 g fat	22 g carbohydrates
1 g saturated fat	7 g fiber
0 mg cholesterol	12 g protein

BRAIN-BOOSTING SMOOTHIES

ENERGIZE & STABILIZE: BREAKFAST

Chapter 3

Did you know that people who eat breakfast every day maintain weight loss better than those who skip their morning meal? Some say it's the most important meal of the day, and I agree. Eating a healthy breakfast that includes protein, essential fats, and complex carbohydrates can give you massive amounts of energy and laser-like focus when you need it most. A good breakfast also helps stabilize your blood sugar and reset your hormones to keep cravings at bay later in the day.

v   ng   gf

Yogurt has been shown to have many health benefits. For example, the live cultures and probiotics in yogurt restore our bodies with many necessary "good bugs." My favorites are raw, organic, unsweetened Greek yogurt or goat's milk yogurt.

Ingredients:

12 ounces organic Greek yogurt or goat's milk yogurt (use rice or coconut yogurt if you are dairy-free)

1 cup fresh blueberries (or other berries of your choice)

1 tablespoon pecans, chopped

1 tablespoon hemp seeds

Optional: 2 tablespoons raw honey or pure maple syrup

Preparation:

1. Divide yogurt into two serving dishes.

2. Top with fresh blueberries.

3. Sprinkle with pecans and hemp seeds.

4. Drizzle with honey or maple syrup if desired and serve. If you use coconut or rice yogurt you will probably not need to sweeten with honey or syrup, as these contain some sugar.

Nutritional information per serving:

210 calories	127 mg sodium
5 g fat	30 g carbohydrates
0 g saturated fat	3 g fiber
0 mg cholesterol	11 g protein

ENERGIZE AND STABILIZE: BREAKFAST

Seafood Omelet for Super Focus

gf **ng**

Ingredients:

2 whole eggs

2 egg whites

5 medium-sized shrimp, peeled, deveined, and halved lengthwise

5 medium-sized scallops

2 teaspoons Earth Balance® or raw organic butter

1 teaspoon coconut oil

1 teaspoon ginger, minced

4 green onions, chopped

½ cup bean sprouts

1 chive, chopped

White pepper

Optional: 1 grapefruit

Preparation:

1. In a skillet, heat oil over medium heat. Add ginger and green onions, and sauté for 1 minute.

2. Add shrimp and scallops, and cook for 1 more minute. Set aside.

3. In a small bowl, whisk egg and egg white, and season with pepper.

4. Heat a medium skillet over medium heat and lightly coat with Earth Balance® or butter. Pour eggs into the skillet. Lift edges frequently to allow uncooked portion to flow underneath. Flip it over and finish cooking, approximately 1 minute.

5. Transfer to plate, top with cooked shrimp, scallops, and bean sprouts. Garnish with chives. Serve with half a grapefruit.

Nutritional information per serving:

325 calories	338 mg sodium
24 g fat	6 g carbohydrates
11 g saturated fat	2 g fiber
249 mg cholesterol	24 g protein

v gf

With the natural sweetness of blueberries and bananas, who needs syrup? These fluffy pancakes do more than just taste great. They contain protein, which helps balance your blood sugar, and they boost your omega-3 intake.

Ingredients:

½ cup buckwheat flour

½ cup gluten-free all purpose baking flour

1 teaspoon baking powder

4 tablespoons ground flax seed

3 tablespoons hemp seeds

2 tablespoons dried blueberries

½ banana, chopped

1¾ cups rice milk

2 tablespoons coconut oil

¼ cup maple syrup

Optional: 2 tablespoons protein powder (highly recommended!)

Preparation:

1. In a medium bowl, mix all dry ingredients.

2. Add blueberries, banana, and milk. Stir until blended well. If it gets too thick, add a little more milk until mixture is smooth and creamy.

3. In a medium skillet, heat oil over medium heat. Spoon the batter onto the skillet, approximately ¼ cup for each pancake.

4. Brown on both sides and serve warm, drizzled with pure maple syrup.

Nutritional information per serving:

256 calories	112 mg sodium
10 g fat	39 g carbohydrates
4 g saturated fat	5 g fiber
0 mg cholesterol	7 g protein

Brainy Breakfast Burrito

Adaptable **veg** *gf* **ng**

In the Amen household, we typically "go green" when we eat burritos. That means we use romaine lettuce leaves as a wrap to increase veggie intake and cut calories. If you prefer a tortilla, try a sprouted-grain version for extra nutritional value.

Ingredients:

1 whole egg

1 egg white

1 teaspoon coconut butter or raw organic butter

1 leek, cut in half moons (white part only)

1 garlic clove, minced

¼ cup red bell pepper, chopped

¼ cup crimini mushrooms, sliced

¼ cup broccoli, chopped

¼ avocado, sliced

1 tablespoon salsa

Romaine/iceberg lettuce leaves or 1 Ezekiel sprouted grain tortilla

Preparation:

1. In a small bowl, whisk egg and egg white.

2. In a medium skillet, heat butter over medium heat.

3. Add leek and garlic, and sauté for 1 minute.

4. Add bell peppers, mushrooms, and broccoli, and cook for 2-3 minutes.

5. Add eggs, and stir until cooked through.

6. Double up romaine leaves and spread with salsa as desired. Top with avocado. Wrap egg mixture in romaine lettuce leaves.

7. If using tortillas, warm in the microwave for 20 seconds. Spread each tortilla with 1 tablespoon of salsa, divide egg mixture, and top with sliced avocado. Roll up and serve immediately.

Nutritional information per serving:

311 calories	218 mg sodium
19 g fat	25 g carbohydrates
3 g saturated fat	7 g fiber
213 mg cholesterol	16 g protein

Tortilla only nutritional information:

150 calories	140 mg sodium
4 g fat	24 g carbohydrates
1 g saturated fat	5 g fiber
0 mg cholesterol	6 g protein

Totally Tofu Scramble

v   gf   ng

Ingredients:

16 ounces silken tofu (firm will give you chunks, soft will give you more of a "scrambled egg" consistency)

1 tablespoon coconut oil

1 leek, chopped in half moons (white part only)

2 green onions, chopped

⅓ cup broccoli, cut in small pieces

⅓ cup red bell pepper, chopped finely

1 tablespoon chives, chopped finely

Garlic salt to taste

Pepper to taste

Preparation:

1. Drain and press liquid out of tofu over a strainer. Break into small pieces.

2. In a medium skillet, heat oil over medium heat. Stir in leeks and green onions, and sauté for 2 minutes.

3. Add broccoli and bell peppers, and cook for 2 minutes.

4. Add tofu for 1 minute or until warmed through. Season with garlic salt and pepper as desired. Serve warm, sprinkled with chives.

Nutritional information per serving:

182 calories	206 mg sodium
9 g fat	11 g carbohydrates
6 g saturated fat	2 g fiber
0 mg cholesterol	16 g protein

Alpha-Omega Oatmeal

v gf

Oatmeal is almost as American as apple pie. This protein-packed version makes for a better-balanced breakfast choice. And thanks to the cinnamon, it can also enhance your attention and help regulate blood sugar levels, which may help curb your cravings.

Ingredients:

1 cup steel-cut oats (Instant oats do not count! You might as well eat sugar!)

2 tablespoons flax seeds

3½ cups water

2 tablespoons protein powder

1 cup almond or rice milk

1 cup blueberries

1 small apple, chopped

2 tablespoons raw walnuts, chopped

Cinnamon

Optional: 10 drops vanilla crème-flavored liquid stevia

Preparation:

1. In a medium pot, mix oats, flax seeds, and water. Bring it to a boil. Cover, reduce heat to low, and simmer. Stir occasionally for 45-50 minutes or until the oats are soft and the mixture is creamy.

2. When oats are cooked, mix in protein powder.

3. Stir in almond milk, blueberries, and chopped apple. Add stevia as needed.

4. Sprinkle with cinnamon.

5. Top with chopped walnuts.

Nutritional information per serving:

247 calories	64 mg sodium
5 g fat	45 g carbohydrates
1 g saturated fat	8 g fiber
0 mg cholesterol	10 g protein

ENERGIZE AND STABILIZE: BREAKFAST

Feel-Good Eggs Ranchero

veg **gf** **ng** Adaptable

Did you know that eggs are good-mood foods? They are high in the building blocks for dopamine, which is the brain's feel-good neurotransmitter. So when you start your day with eggs, it can put a little extra spring in your step. Personally, I love this meal because of the balance between protein and carbs.

Ingredients:

1 whole egg

1 egg white

2 teaspoons coconut oil

2 shallots, chopped

1 garlic clove, minced

½ cup red or kidney beans (Always soak overnight and cook thoroughly. Use canned if you prefer.)

¼ teaspoon cumin

½ teaspoon paprika

2 cups baby spinach or 2 gluten-free tortillas

2 tablespoons fire-roasted salsa

Salt and pepper to taste

Optional: ½ teaspoon garlic salt

Preparation:

1. In a medium skillet, heat 1 teaspoon coconut oil over medium heat. Sauté shallots and garlic for 3 minutes.

2. Add beans, cumin, garlic salt, and paprika, and season with pepper as desired. Cook for 4 minutes, stirring frequently. Set aside and keep it warm.

3. Heat the rest of the coconut oil in a small skillet and cook eggs until no longer opaque. Season with salt and pepper.

4. Place the spinach on a plate. Top with beans and eggs, and serve with salsa.

Nutritional information per serving:

306 calories	405 mg sodium
17 g fat	30 g carbohydrates
13 g saturated fat	4 g fiber
106 mg cholesterol	13 g protein

ENERGIZE AND STABILIZE: BREAKFAST

51

LIGHT & LUSCIOUS: LUNCHES

Chapter 4

Never allowing yourself to get too hungry is one of the keys to success when you are trying to lose weight. When you go too long without eating, your blood sugar levels can crash. Having low blood sugar will cause you to be impulsive and more likely to make poor food choices. Eating small, frequent meals that include vegetables, protein, and healthy fats will keep your metabolism "revved." The lunch recipes here are light in calories and high in nutritional value to keep you energized throughout the afternoon.

Shirataki noodles: We recommend these noodles so often as an alternative that we have listed the cooking instructions on this page as a reference. Don't prepare them according to the package - they are not very tasty that way. This is how we find them to be the most appealing.

**Boil water in a pot. Empty and drain Shirataki noodles from package. You may want to cut noodles before boiling. Add to boiling water. Reduce heat and simmer for 3 minutes. Drain the noodles well (they tend to retain water).

LIGHT & LUSCIOUS: LUNCHES

Get Happy Grilled Halibut with Vegetables

Makes 4 Servings

gf ng

Ingredients for Halibut:

4 halibut fillets (4-6 ounces each)

1 tablespoon grape seed oil

1 lime, juiced

2 tablespoons cilantro, chopped

¼ teaspoon salt

¼ teaspoon pepper

Ingredients for Grilled Vegetables:

1 tablespoon coconut oil

1 red onion, julienned or cut into strips

2 garlic cloves, minced

1 zucchini, cut in long strips

1 yellow pepper, sliced

20 grape tomatoes, halved

2 tablespoons basil, chopped

Salt and pepper to taste

Preparation for Halibut:

1. Combine oil, lime juice, cilantro, salt, and pepper in plastic bag.

2. Add halibut, seal, and turn to coat.

3. Refrigerate for 30 minutes to 1 hour.

4. Preheat the grill to high heat.

5. Grill fish for about 5 minutes on each side, until it flakes with a fork.

Preparation for Vegetables:

1. In a large skillet heat oil over medium heat.

2. Add onions, and sauté for 3 minutes. Add garlic, and sauté for 1 more minute.

3. Stir in zucchini and yellow peppers. Cover and simmer for 3 minutes.

4. Add tomatoes and basil, and sauté for 4 minutes.

5. Season with salt and pepper.

6. Spoon vegetables on plate, and serve fish over vegetables. Garnish with basil.

Nutritional information per serving:

256 calories	230 mg sodium
10 g fat	9 g carbohydrates
4 g saturated fat	2 g fiber
46 mg cholesterol	32 g protein

Halibut only nutritional information:

191 calories	224 mg sodium
7 g fat	1 g carbohydrates
1 g saturated fat	1 g fiber
46 mg cholesterol	30 g protein

Chicken Vegetable Wrap

Makes 4 Servings

Adaptable gf ng

Ingredients:

2 boneless, skinless chicken breasts (4-6 ounces each), sliced

2 tablespoons fresh lime juice

2 tablespoons cilantro, chopped

1 tablespoon grape seed oil

4 tablespoons Vegenaise®

1 teaspoon curry powder

1 teaspoon fresh lime juice

¼ teaspoon pepper

2 cups baby spinach

1 avocado, sliced

1 cup low-sodium salsa

Romaine/iceberg lettuce leaves or 4 Ezekiel sprouted grain tortillas (or gluten-free tortillas)

Optional: ½ teaspoon garlic salt

Preparation:

1. In a large bowl, combine cilantro, 2 tablespoons of lime juice and garlic salt (if desired).

2. Add chicken. Cover and refrigerate for 1-2 hours.

3. In a small bowl, combine Vegenaise®, curry powder, pepper, and 1 teaspoon of lime juice. Set aside.

4. In a large pan, heat oil on medium-high heat. Add chicken strips, and cook until browned and cooked through, about 10 minutes.

5. If using tortillas, microwave for about 20 seconds. Spread wrap of your choice with curry sauce. Divide ingredients evenly, spreading a thin layer of spinach, chicken, and avocado down the middle of each wrap. Fold two sides of wrap over filling, then roll tightly, ending seam side down. Cut in half diagonally. Serve with salsa as desired.

Nutritional information per serving:

474 calories	1044 mg sodium
27 g fat	35 g carbohydrates
1 g saturated fat	25 g fiber
66 mg cholesterol	43 g protein

Tortilla only nutritional information:

150 calories	140 mg sodium
3.5 g fat	24 g carbohydrates
1 g saturated fat	5 g fiber
0 mg cholesterol	6 g protein

Savory Lubian Rose Stew

v **gf** **ng** **Adaptable**

Makes 4 Servings

I love the versatility of this recipe. Whether you are a protein lover or a vegetarian, you can adapt this recipe to fit your needs. It is simple, tasty, and nutritious.

Ingredients:

12 ounces lean grass-fed, antibiotic-free, hormone-free lamb, chopped into bite-sized pieces

½ cup brown rice (substitute rice with barley... or skip it altogether!)

1 tablespoon refined coconut oil or grape seed oil

¼ teaspoon salt

¼ teaspoon pepper

½ teaspoon cinnamon

½ small onion, chopped

1 28-ounce can diced tomatoes (fresh if you have time)

2 cups fresh green beans

Optional: 2 tablespoons pine nuts

Optional: Vegetarians may substitute lamb with Tempeh, or no meat. Try topping it with a few extra pine nuts.

Optional: For the "Paleo," grain-free version of this meal, skip the rice and just eat the lamb and veggies with the pine nuts.

Preparation:

1. Place rice in 1 cup boiling water. Add salt, pepper, and cinnamon. Cook according to time on package, approximately 20 minutes.

2. In a medium-large pan, heat oil over medium heat. Add onions, and sauté for 1 minute.

3. Add lamb and cook until meat is lightly browned on all sides, about 5-7 minutes. Turn regularly.

4. Add tomatoes and pepper. Lower heat, cover, and simmer for 15 minutes.

5. Add green beans and simmer for another 5 minutes.

6. Place rice on serving platter and serve lamb and tomato mixture over the top. Sprinkle with pine nuts if desired. Serve with a green salad.

Nutritional information per serving:

393 calories	303 mg sodium
23 g fat	22 g carbohydrates
11 g saturated fat	6 g fiber
85 mg cholesterol	25 g protein

Seared Ahi with Cucumber Salad

Makes 2 Servings

This quick and nutritious meal is one of our favorites. It is perfectly satisfying.

Ingredients:

2 ahi tuna steaks (4-6 ounces each)

2 teaspoons coconut oil

1 lime, juiced

2 garlic cloves, minced

2 teaspoons fresh ginger, grated

1 teaspoon honey

4 Persian cucumbers, thinly sliced

½ avocado, diced

1 tablespoon olive oil

2 teaspoons dill, chopped

1 shallot, finely chopped

1 teaspoon fresh lemon juice

3 cups mixed greens

Salt and pepper to taste

Preparation for Cucumber Salad:

1. In a medium bowl, combine cucumber, avocado, olive oil, dill, shallots, and lemon juice, and season with salt and pepper.

2. Cover and refrigerate for 30 minutes.

Preparation for Tuna:

1. In a medium bowl, mix lime juice, garlic, ginger, and honey.

2. Season tuna with salt and pepper. Place fish in lime marinade, cover, and refrigerate for 15-30 minutes.

3. In a skillet, heat coconut oil over medium heat. Sear tuna for 1-2 minutes on each side (depending on how rare you prefer). Remove from pan and slice into ¼-inch thick slices.

4. Dish cucumber salad on plates with tuna.

Nutritional information per serving:

361 calories	60 mg sodium
6 g fat	20 g carbohydrates
13 g saturated fat	7 g fiber
50 mg cholesterol	31 g protein

Tasty Turkey Wrap

It doesn't get easier than this when you are on the run.

Ingredients:

½ pound free-range, antibiotic-free, hormone-free turkey, sliced

2 cups mixed baby greens

2 tomatoes, sliced

1 small avocado, sliced

2 tablespoons olive oil

1 teaspoon fresh lime juice

2 tablespoons fresh cilantro, chopped

Salt and pepper to taste

Romaine/iceberg lettuce leaves or 4 Ezekiel sprouted grain tortillas (or gluten-free)

Preparation:

1. In a large bowl, combine olive oil, lemon juice, cilantro, salt, and pepper.

2. Add baby greens and mix well.

3. Divide turkey among tortillas.

4. Top with baby greens, tomatoes, and avocado.

5. Fold the wrap over about 1-inch on two opposite sides, and then roll up completely. Slice in half diagonally and serve.

Nutritional information per serving:

223 calories	492 mg sodium
18 g fat	9 g carbohydrates
3 g saturated fat	4 g fiber
24 mg cholesterol	10 g protein

Tortilla only nutritional information:

150 calories	140 mg sodium
3.5 g fat	24 g carbohydrates
1 g saturated fat	5 g fiber
0 mg cholesterol	6 g protein

Very Veggie Pita

v gf

Ingredients:

2 gluten-free pitas

2 tablespoons Vegenaise®

2 garlic cloves, minced

1 teaspoon fresh marjoram, chopped

3 tablespoons hemp seeds

1 Persian cucumber, sliced

1 cup alfalfa sprouts

2 green onions, thinly sliced

1 tomato, sliced

½ avocado, sliced

1 cup romaine lettuce, shredded

4 tablespoons hummus

Preparation:

1. In a small bowl, mix Vegenaise®, garlic, marjoram, and hemp seeds.

2. Wrap pita bread in paper towel and microwave for 30 seconds or until soft and slightly warm.

3. Spread pita bread with Vegenaise® sauce and fill each with half of vegetables.

4. Top each with hummus.

Nutritional information per serving:

490 calories	446 mg sodium
25 g fat	51 g carbohydrates
1 g saturated fat	11 g fiber
0 mg cholesterol	18 g protein

Amazing Apple Cinnamon Chicken Salad

Makes 2 Servings

gf　ng

Ingredients:

2 boneless, skinless chicken breasts (4-6 ounces)

1 medium apple, chopped

½ cup raisins

2 tablespoons Vegenaise®

1 teaspoon apple cider vinegar

½ teaspoon cinnamon

2 tablespoons pecans, chopped

4 cups of lettuce

¼ teaspoon pepper

Optional: ½ teaspoon salt

Preparation:

1. Preheat the grill to medium-high heat.
2. Season chicken with salt and pepper as desired.
3. Cook chicken 7-10 minutes on each side or until the juices run clear. Let it cool.
4. In a medium bowl, mix Vegenaise®, vinegar, and cinnamon.
5. Dice chicken into large chunks.
6. Add chicken, apple, and raisins to dressing mixture.
7. Toss gently to coat. Season with salt and pepper if needed.
8. Refrigerate for 2 hours. Serve on a bed of your favorite greens.

Nutritional information per serving:

283 calories	107 mg sodium
11 g fat	25 g carbohydrates
2 g saturated fat	4 g fiber
49 mg cholesterol	22 g protein

Teriyaki Rice Bowl with Salmon

Makes 2 Servings

Adaptable **gf** **ng**

This dish is traditionally eaten with rice, but you can easily make it a grain-free dish by serving the salmon over greens.

Ingredients:

2 salmon steaks (4-6 ounces each)

1 cup brown rice, cooked

4 teaspoons tamari sauce

1 tablespoon rice vinegar

1 teaspoon ginger, grated

1 teaspoon honey

1 garlic clove, minced

¼ teaspoon cayenne pepper

1 tablespoon sesame oil

1 teaspoon Dijon mustard

2 tablespoons fresh cilantro, chopped

½ cup carrots, grated

⅓ cup scallions, chopped

Radicchio leaves

Preparation:

1. Preheat oven to 400 degrees F.

2. In a medium bowl, mix tamari sauce, rice vinegar, ginger, honey, garlic, and cayenne pepper. Transfer salmon steaks to a baking dish and cover with marinade.

3. Refrigerate for 15-30 minutes.

4. In a large bowl, mix sesame oil, mustard, and cilantro.

5. Stir in cooked rice, carrots, and scallions.

6. Roast salmon for about 15 minutes or until fish flakes with fork. Arrange radicchio on a plate and top with rice salad and salmon.

Nutritional information per serving:

539 calories	373 mg sodium
18 g fat	59 g carbohydrates
3 g saturated fat	6 g fiber
80 mg cholesterol	36 g protein

Warm Chicken Wraps

Makes 2 Servings

Ingredients:

2 free-range, antibiotic-free, hormone-free, boneless, skinless chicken breasts (4-6 ounces each), cut into thin strips

2 teaspoons grape seed oil

1 tablespoon ginger, finely grated

2 teaspoons sesame oil

2 garlic cloves, minced

1 tablespoon rice vinegar

½ teaspoon crushed red pepper flakes

2 tablespoons dried cranberries

1 8-ounce can water chestnuts, drained and sliced

2 tablespoons cashews or walnuts, roughly chopped

1 cup bean sprouts

3 green onions, chopped

1 tablespoon black sesame seeds

1 head romaine/iceberg lettuce leaves, separated

Optional: 2 teaspoons tamari sauce (this tastes great, but increases the sodium substantially)

Preparation:

1. In a large bowl, combine grape seed oil, ginger, sesame oil, garlic, tamari sauce, rice vinegar, and red pepper flakes.

2. Add chicken strips and refrigerate for 2 hours.

3. Heat a skillet over medium-high heat. Stir in chicken with marinade and cook for 3-4 minutes. Add 1-2 tablespoons of water if necessary to prevent drying and sticking.

4. Add cranberries and cook for another minute.

5. Add chestnuts and cashews and stir to warm.

6. Meanwhile, arrange whole lettuce leaves on a plate. Fill lettuce with chicken mixture.

7. Top with bean sprouts, green onions, and sprinkle with sesame seeds.

Nutritional information per serving:

461 calories	97 mg sodium
22 g fat	36 g carbohydrates
4 g saturated fat	6 g fiber
66 mg cholesterol	34 g protein

Pasta Pomodoro

Makes 4 Servings

v · gf · ng

Since there are virtually no calories in this dish, add grilled shrimp or chicken for more sustenance, or eat it with a large salad topped with nuts or seeds.

Ingredients:

16 ounces Shirataki noodles (You may use whole-wheat noodles instead, but they increase your carb load and are not figured into the calorie count.)

2 tablespoons coconut oil

½ cup shallots, sliced

3 garlic cloves, minced

8 Roma tomatoes, diced

1 teaspoon lemon pepper

2 tablespoons fresh basil, chopped

2 tablespoons fresh parsley, chopped

1 tablespoon hemp seed oil

Salt to taste

Optional: 16 ounces grilled shrimp or chicken

Preparation:

1. In a large pot, bring water to a boil. Put noodles in boiling water, reduce heat, and simmer for 2-3 minutes.

2. Meanwhile, heat coconut oil in a large skillet over medium heat. Add shallots and cook for 2 minutes. Add garlic and cook for 1 more minute.

3. Add tomatoes and simmer for 4 minutes.

4. When pasta is warmed through, drain it well and add it to the skillet with tomatoes.

5. Season with salt and lemon pepper. Add basil and parsley. Toss gently.

6. Serve drizzled with hemp seed oil and grilled shrimp or chicken and a large green salad.

Nutritional information per serving:

167 calories	32 mg sodium
12 g fat	15 g carbohydrates
6 g saturated fat	5 g fiber
0 mg cholesterol	3 g protein

Barley Veggie Bowl with Sweet Potatoes

Makes 2 Servings

It's so much better than your average "bowl." You won't find a more satisfying lunch anywhere. Barley is a low-glycemic, low-cost dynamo that fills you up for hours. Plus, this smart meal choice features turmeric (found in the curry), which may help protect against Alzheimer's disease.

Ingredients:

2 tablespoons vegetable broth, for sautéing (or 1 teaspoon coconut oil)

1 onion, chopped

2 garlic cloves, minced

1 medium sweet potato, peeled and diced

¼ cup barley

1 teaspoon fresh ginger, grated

1 tablespoon raisins

1 teaspoon curry

½ teaspoon cinnamon

2 cups vegetable broth

2 cups broccoli florets

4 ounces firm tofu, cubed

1 tablespoon cilantro, chopped

Salt and pepper to taste

Preparation:

1. In a large pot, heat vegetable broth or oil over medium heat. Add onion and sauté for 2 minutes.

2. Stir in garlic and cook for 1 more minute.

3. Add barley, ginger, raisins, curry, cinnamon, and vegetable broth. Bring it to a boil. Lower heat and simmer for 20 minutes.

4. Add sweet potatoes and cook for 10 more minutes or until barley is cooked, stirring occasionally.

5. Stir in broccoli, tofu, and cilantro. Cook for 2-3 minutes.

6. Season with salt and pepper. Serve warm.

Nutritional information per serving:

403 calories	190 mg sodium
3 g fat	84 g carbohydrates
0 g saturated fat	24 g fiber
0 mg cholesterol	11 g protein

Get Smart Mahi Mahi Burger with Pineapple Salsa

Makes 4 Servings

Adaptable gf ng

Ingredients for Halibut:

4 mahi mahi fillets (4 ounces each)

1 tablespoon grape seed oil

1 cup fresh pineapple, diced

½ cup red bell pepper, diced

2 tablespoons fresh cilantro, minced

2 tablespoons shallots, minced

Large romaine/iceberg lettuce leaves or Oroweat Multi-Grain Sandwich Thins® (only 100 calories)

Lemon pepper

Salt and pepper to taste

Preparation for Halibut:

1. Preheat the grill to medium-high heat.

2. Brush fillets with oil and sprinkle with lemon pepper.

3. Grill fillets for about 5 minutes per side or until mahi mahi flakes easily when tested with fork. Serve on romaine leaves or buns with pineapple salsa.

Preparation for Pineapple Salsa:

4. Mix pineapple, red bell pepper, cilantro, and shallots, and season with salt and pepper.

Nutritional information per serving:

257 calories	336 mg sodium
5 g fat	30 g carbohydrates
4 g saturated fat	5 g fiber
40 mg cholesterol	27 g protein

Portobello Burger

v

These vegan burgers are so hearty, you won't miss the beef, mayo, and bun. Try them a few times, and you'll never want a fast-food burger again.

Ingredients:

4 portobello mushroom caps

2 tablespoons grape seed oil

2 tablespoons red wine vinegar

2 garlic cloves, minced

1 tablespoon fresh oregano

4 thin burger buns (I recommend Oroweat Multi-Grain Sandwich Thins®)

1 cup arugula

½ red onion, julienned

1 avocado, sliced

1 tablespoon pine nuts

Salt and pepper

Optional: 2 tablespoons feta or goat cheese (vegans may opt for nut or soy cheese)

Preparation:

1. In a small bowl, whisk oil, vinegar, garlic, and oregano.

2. Brush mushroom caps with marinade. Set aside for 10-20 minutes.

3. Preheat the grill to medium heat.

4. Grill mushrooms for 3 minutes on each side or until tender.

5. Season with salt and pepper. Place on warm, toasted buns.

6. Top with arugula, red onion, avocado, pine nuts, and feta cheese (if desired).

Nutritional information per serving:

282 calories	242 mg sodium
16 g fat	33 g carbohydrates
2 g saturated fat	10 g fiber
0 mg cholesterol	9 g protein

LIGHT AND LUSCIOUS: LUNCHES

Keen Quinoa Pilaf

IIIIIIIIIIIIIIIIIIIIIIIIIIIIIIIIIIIIIIIIIIIIIIIIIIIIIIIIIIIIIIIIIIIIIIIIIIIIIIIIIIIIIIIIIIIIIIIIIIIIIII

Makes 6 Servings

gf   v

Quinoa is one of my favorite "whole grains" for vegetarians because it is gluten-free and has a bit more protein than most other sources of grains.

Ingredients:

1 cup quinoa

½ cup red lentils

2 cups vegetable broth

¼ cup fresh parsley, chopped

2 tablespoons pine nuts

Salt and pepper to taste

Preparation:

1. Rinse quinoa well. Combine quinoa, red lentils, and vegetable broth in a medium saucepan. Bring to a boil over high heat. Lower heat, cover, and simmer for 20 minutes or until quinoa is fluffy.

2. Stir in parsley and pine nuts. Season with salt and pepper. Serve with steamed vegetables.

Nutritional information per serving:

159 calories	49 mg sodium
4 g fat	26 g carbohydrates
0 g saturated fat	4 g fiber
0 mg cholesterol	6 g protein

Soba Noodles with Vegetables and "Peanut" Sauce

Makes 6 Servings

Adaptable ▽ v ◇ gf ● ng

This gluten-free, vegetarian recipe can be adapted for non-vegetarians by replacing soba noodles with Shirataki noodles and adding shrimp. The delectable "peanut" sauce in this recipe actually comes from cashew butter, which offers far more nutritional benefits than peanut butter. Your guests will never know it's not peanut butter.

Ingredients:

16 ounces soba (buckwheat) noodles or Shirataki noodles

¼ cup grape seed oil

½ cup raw cashew butter, smooth (use peanut butter, if you must)

2 tablespoons tahini

2 garlic cloves, minced

1 tablespoon fresh ginger, minced

3 tablespoons tamari sauce

1 tablespoon sesame oil

¼ cup rice vinegar

1 tablespoon fresh lime juice

⅓ cup light coconut milk

1 red bell pepper, cut in thin strips

1 green bell pepper, cut in thin strips

1 carrot, julienned

6 ounces firm tofu

1 cup organic edamame

6 green onions, chopped

1 tablespoon cilantro

1 tablespoon sesame seeds

Optional: 4-6 ounces shrimp, deveined and cooked

Preparation:

1. In a blender bowl or food processor place oil, nut butter, tahini, garlic, ginger, tamari sauce, sesame oil, rice vinegar, lime juice, and coconut milk. Purée until smooth. Transfer to a large bowl.

2. Fill the bottom of a large pot with water and place a steamer basket in the bottom. Do not cover the steamer basket with water. Place peppers, carrots, and tofu in the basket and cover. Steam vegetables and tofu for 2 minutes.

3. Meanwhile, boil a large pot of water and cook soba noodles according to cooking directions on package. Drain pasta and add directly to a bowl with "peanut" sauce.

4. If using Shirataki noodles and shrimp option: Drain noodles from liquid in package. Boil water, add noodles, and simmer for 3 minutes. Warm shrimp in a pot or add to steamed veggies to warm. Drain water from noodles well (they retain water), and then add noodles to "peanut" sauce. Go to step five.

5. Stir in steamed vegetables, tofu, edamame, and green onions. Toss well. Serve sprinkled with cilantro and sesame seeds.

Nutritional information per serving:

362 calories	541 mg sodium
28 g fat	19 g carbohydrates
5 g saturated fat	4 g fiber
0 mg cholesterol	12 g protein

Avocado Wrap

ng   gf   v   **Adaptable**

This may be a vegan meal, but you don't have to be a vegan to love it. With avocado, hummus, bell peppers, and bean sprouts, what's not to love? I prefer it with lettuce leaves for wraps. Go ahead and give it a try. What have you got to lose, except maybe a few pounds?

Ingredients:

Romaine/iceberg lettuce leaves or 2 Ezekiel sprouted grain tortillas or rice tortillas

1 tablespoon grape seed oil

2 tablespoons hummus or split-pea hummus (see page 178).

1 avocado, sliced

1 cup watercress

2 roasted red bell peppers (you can use raw if desired)

1 cup bean sprouts

1 tablespoon hemp seeds

Salt and pepper to taste

Preparation:

1. Preheat the grill to medium-high heat (if roasting peppers). Put peppers in a plastic bag and drizzle with grape seed oil. Turn bag until peppers are lightly coated with oil.

2. Grill peppers on all sides until grill marks begin to appear. Place into paper bag or glass bowl and cover with plastic wrap. Let peppers steam for 15 minutes.

3. Remove from bag or bowl, pull the stems out of peppers, and gently peel the skin off. Slice into thick strips.

4. Warm tortillas in microwave for 30 seconds.

5. Spread tortillas with hummus, then layer watercress, pepper strips, and avocado in the center. Top with bean sprouts.

6. Sprinkle with hemp seeds.

7. Season with salt and pepper. Fold in sides and roll tightly.

Nutritional information per serving:

504 calories	249 mg sodium
30 g fat	50 g carbohydrates
3 g saturated fat	16 g fiber
0 mg cholesterol	15 g protein

Simple Shrimp Scampi

ng   **gf**

Kids usually love this simple recipe and it tastes great alone over Shirataki noodles. The coconut flavor is a fresh alternative to traditional scampi.

Ingredients:

1 pound raw large shrimp, peeled and deveined

1 tablespoon coconut oil

1 teaspoon garlic, minced

1 teaspoon oregano, chopped

1 teaspoon basil, chopped

½ cup light coconut milk

1 teaspoon fresh lemon juice

Optional: ½ teaspoon crushed red pepper flakes

Preparation:

1. In a skillet, heat coconut oil over medium heat.

2. Add red pepper flakes. Cook for 1 minute.

3. Add shrimp, and cook for 1 minute on both sides, just until they turn pink. Be careful not to overcook.

4. Add garlic, oregano, and basil.

5. Stir in coconut milk and lemon juice. Cook until slightly thickened, about 1 minute.

6. Serve over favorite greens or Shirataki noodles.

Nutritional information per serving:

102 calories	76 mg sodium
6 g fat	3 g carbohydrates
5 g saturated fat	0 g fiber
66 mg cholesterol	10 g protein

Kobe Beef and Shirataki Noodles- Daniel's Favorite 10-Minute Meal

Makes 2 Servings

ng **gf**

My husband has many talents and gifts, but cooking is not one of them. So when he decided to surprise me with dinner one night, I was a little worried, especially when he came out of the kitchen only 10 minutes later! But it was delicious! And it followed all of our principles, so his recipe made the cookbook.

Ingredients:

8 ounces lean grass-fed, antibiotic-free Kobe beef, chopped into bite-sized pieces (have the butcher do this to save time)

16 ounces Shirataki noodles

2 teaspoons coconut oil or grape seed oil

1½ cup organic low-sodium tomato pasta sauce

Garlic salt to taste

Pepper to taste

Herbs of your choice

Preparation:

1. Season meat with salt, pepper, and herbs as desired.

2. Heat oil in large skillet. Brown meat on all sides, about 3-4 minutes.

3. Add tomato sauce, cover and simmer for 5-7 minutes.

4. Meanwhile, bring water to a boil in a medium pot. Drain noodles from liquid in package. You may want to cut noodles before boiling. Put noodles in boiling water, reduce heat, and simmer for 3 minutes.

5. When noodles are finished simmering, remove from water, and drain well. Shirataki noodles retain water and will make your sauce thin if you don't get all the water out.

6. Stir noodles into meat sauce. Serve with a large green salad or steamed veggies.

Nutritional information per serving:

372 calories	212 mg sodium
26 g fat	13 g carbohydrates
12 g saturated fat	2 g fiber
74 mg cholesterol	26 g protein

RELAX AND REJUVENATE: DINNERS

Chapter 5

Chapter 5

By now you've eaten several small meals. Hopefully you had a productive day and didn't feel deprived. If so, you probably need to take a look at your journal (you are journaling, right?) and assess your snacks. You may need to add a snack. While in the weight loss phase of your program, a snack of raw, unsalted nuts and a small apple in the mid afternoon can help tremendously. Nuts help prevent the breakdown of muscle when you are losing weight, and they provide healthy fat while giving you focus.

Dinnertime is the time to reflect on your progress and accomplishment for the day. Celebrate your success and plan for the next day. Do not beat yourself up if you were not perfect. Perfection is an excuse not to succeed, or to put forth serious effort.

Give thanks and fill your mind with gratitude. You are far more likely to succeed from a place of gratitude.

Pan-Roasted Salmon with Vegetables

Makes 4 Servings

gf ng

Ingredients:

4 salmon fillets (4-6 ounces each)

2 tablespoons coconut oil

1 onion, chopped

2 garlic cloves, minced

1 fennel bulb, cored and cut into strips

20 plump asparagus spears, woodsy ends removed

2 pinches saffron threads, crushed

2 cups fresh diced tomatoes (or 1 14.5-ounce can diced tomatoes in a pinch)

½ cup vegetable stock

2 tablespoons basil, chopped

Salt and pepper to taste

Preparation:

1. Sprinkle salmon with salt and pepper.

2. In a large skillet, heat oil over medium-high heat.

3. Sear salmon for about 1 minute per side (don't cook it through). Transfer to a plate.

4. Add onion and garlic to same skillet, and sauté for 4 minutes.

5. Stir in fennel, asparagus, and saffron. Stir to coat, and cook for 4 minutes.

6. Add tomatoes and vegetable stock. Season with salt and pepper, cover and simmer for about 5 minutes.

7. Return fish to pan. Sprinkle with basil, cover, and cook for 3 minutes or until fish is cooked through.

8. Transfer salmon to a plate. Spoon vegetable mixture over fish, and serve.

9. Garnish with fresh basil.

Nutritional information per serving:

339 calories	159 mg sodium
16 g fat	17 g carbohydrates
7 g saturated fat	6 g fiber
80 mg cholesterol	33 g protein

You'll Never Know It's Vegetarian Chili

Most people who try this have no idea it is a vegetarian dish. It is one of my favorites! I especially love it because of the amount of luscious vegetables included. Believe it or not, even my seven-year-old daughter can't detect the vegetables. But a word of caution if you are gluten-sensitive: most meat substitutes contain gluten.

Ingredients:

4 Boca® burgers (for vegetarians)

1 onion, diced

2 garlic cloves, minced

1 tablespoon refined coconut oil

1 small can Ortega® chiles

1 tablespoon fresh oregano

1 tablespoon chili powder

3 cups tomatoes, peeled and seeded (you may use strained tomatoes from a can if you don't have time to peel and seed fresh tomatoes)

1 cup vegetable broth

1 cup kidney beans, cooked (you may use canned if you don't have time to cook beans)

1 cup black beans or chickpea beans, cooked

3 cups mixed vegetables: ½ cup red bell pepper, ½ cup yellow bell pepper, ½ cup carrots, ½ cup zucchini, ½ cup squash, ½ cup crumbled cauliflower (Be creative! If you prefer other vegetables, feel free to add them.)

1-2 teaspoons salt

Optional: 1 jalapeno pepper (makes chili pretty spicy)

Preparation:

1. In a large cast-iron saucepan or pot heat oil over medium heat. Sauté onions and garlic for about 2 minutes.

2. Add Boca® burgers. Crumble and brown burgers, breaking apart as much as possible.

3. Add jalapeno (if using), chili powder, chiles, oregano, salt, and tomatoes. Mix thoroughly until spices are blended well.

4. Add broth.

5. Dish out 2 cups of chili mixture. Put 1 cup of chili at a time into blender. Add ¾ cup of vegetables at a time into blender, and purée. Pour mixture back into the pot. Add beans. Stir thoroughly and heat through on medium-low heat, about 5 minutes. Serve hot.

Nutritional information per serving:

150 calories	580 mg sodium
3 g fat	23 g carbohydrates
2 g saturated fat	8 g fiber
7 mg cholesterol	12 g protein

RELAX AND REJUVENATE: DINNERS

The Smart Person's "Spaghetti"—Vegetarian Version

ng gf

Makes 4 Servings

Ingredients:

1 large spaghetti squash

1 tablespoon refined coconut oil

1 small yellow onion, chopped

1-2 garlic cloves, minced or pressed

4 medium vine-ripened tomatoes, diced

1 8-ounce can tomato sauce

½ cup zucchini, chopped

⅓ cup red bell pepper, chopped

1½ tablespoons fresh basil, finely chopped (or 1 tablespoon dried)

1½ tablespoons fresh oregano, finely chopped (or 1 tablespoon dried)

1 tablespoon tomato paste, dissolved in ¼ cup vegetable broth or water

¼ teaspoon pepper

Optional: 1 tablespoon sea salt

Optional: ½ cup mushrooms, sliced

Optional: 1 teaspoon corn starch dissolved in ¼ cup soy creamer (add at the end for thicker sauce)

Preparation:

1. Preheat oven to 375 degrees F.

2. Cut spaghetti squash in half and clean out seeds. Place squash face down on a baking dish and bake in oven for about 45 minutes.

3. While squash is baking, heat oil in a large skillet and sauté onions, garlic, and zucchini for 3 minutes over medium heat.

4. Add red bell peppers and mushrooms and sauté for 1 minute.

5. Add remaining ingredients, except water, and simmer over low heat until squash is finished.

6. Monitor sauce for consistency to determine amount of water to be added. Add water as needed.

7. If you prefer a slightly thicker consistency to your sauce, add cornstarch dissolved in soy cream. It won't really change the flavor much, but it will thicken the sauce a bit.

8. When the squash is finished, let it cool for 5 minutes. Use a fork to scoop out the spaghetti squash into a bowl. Squash is finished when fork goes in easily and shreds squash like spaghetti.

9. Spoon sauce over "spaghetti" and serve hot. Serve with a large salad and vegetable dish.

Nutritional information per serving:

139 calories	302 mg sodium
4 g fat	25 g carbohydrates
3 g saturated fat	7 g fiber
0 mg cholesterol	4 g protein

RELAX AND REJUVENATE: DINNERS

OMG! That's all I can say about this one! This is another dish that is great with just a big salad or served over Shirataki noodles (see page 54 for cooking instructions).

Ingredients:

1½ pounds grass-fed, antibiotic-free beef sirloin, cut into bite-sized pieces

3 tablespoons coconut oil

1 onion, julienned

2 garlic cloves, minced

8 ounces crimini mushrooms, sliced

1 teaspoon paprika

1 bay leaf

1 teaspoon garlic salt

1 tablespoon fresh rosemary, chopped

2 cups vegetable broth

1 tablespoon fresh parsley, chopped

¾ cup soy creamer or coconut creamer (coconut creamer may slightly change the taste, but it doesn't have the lectins that are found in soy creamer)

1 tablespoon arrowroot

Salt and pepper to taste

Preparation:

1. In a heavy-bottomed pan, heat 2 tablespoons of coconut oil over medium heat. Add onions and sauté for 3 minutes.

2. Add garlic and sauté for 1 more minute. Transfer the onion and garlic to a bowl.

3. In the same pan, cook mushrooms for 5 minutes. Set mushrooms aside with onions and garlic.

4. In the same pan, add the rest of coconut oil and beef. Sprinkle with paprika. Cook for 3-5 minutes or until the meat is browned on all sides.

5. Add onion, garlic, mushrooms, and rosemary to the beef.

6. Stir in vegetable broth, season with salt and pepper as desired, and cover. Bring to a boil, reduce heat, and simmer for 50 minutes or until meat is tender.

7. Meanwhile, in a small bowl, mix the soy creamer and arrowroot. When meat is cooked, add it to the pan. Simmer for 3 minutes. Stir in parsley and serve. Be sure to serve with a large salad or vegetable dish.

Nutritional information per serving:

340 calories	303 mg sodium
18 g fat	7 g carbohydrates
9 g saturated fat	1 g fiber
100 mg cholesterol	35 g protein

RELAX AND REJUVENATE: DINNERS

Indian-Style Chicken

gf   ng

This is very mildly spiced. It passed the "child taste test" in our house and quickly became a favorite.

Ingredients:

2 boneless, skinless chicken breasts (4-6 ounces each), cut into bite-sized pieces

1 tablespoon coconut oil

1 onion, chopped

3 garlic cloves, minced

½ teaspoon cinnamon

1 bay leaf

¼ teaspoon cloves

2 teaspoons ground cumin

1½ teaspoons ground coriander

3 tomatoes, chopped

4 cups baby spinach

½ green chili, chopped

1 tablespoon fresh lemon juice

Salt and white pepper to taste

Preparation:

1. In a large pot, bring water to a boil. Cook the spinach for 1 minute and transfer to ice-cold water. Drain water.

2. Purée spinach in a blender with the green chili. Set aside.

3. Heat the oil in pan. Add cinnamon, bay leaf, cloves, cumin, and coriander. Cook for 1 minute, stirring constantly.

4. Add the onions, and cook for 3 minutes.

5. Add garlic and cook for additional minute.

6. Stir in the chicken and cook for 5 minutes.

7. Stir in tomatoes and cook for 5 more minutes.

8. Add spinach purée and lemon juice.

9. Season with salt and pepper.

10. Mix well and simmer for about 5 minutes or until the chicken is tender.

11. Serve over greens or brown rice.

Nutritional information per serving:

281 calories	162 mg sodium
10 g fat	20 g carbohydrates
6 g saturated fat	6 g fiber
66 mg cholesterol	31 g protein

My husband loves this recipe with the spaghetti squash. But if you are really trying to lose weight, try it with Shirataki noodles (see page 54 for cooking instructions).

Ingredients:

1 large spaghetti squash or Shirataki noodles

1 pound free-range, antibiotic-free ground turkey

1 tablespoon coconut oil

1 onion, chopped

3 garlic cloves, minced

3 tablespoons tomato paste

2 cups fresh diced tomatoes (or 1 14.5-ounce can chopped tomatoes in a pinch)

2 cups vegetable broth

4 ounces crimini mushrooms, sliced

1 tablespoon fresh oregano, chopped

1 tablespoon fresh basil, chopped

½ cup soy creamer or coconut creamer (We always prefer coconut creamer, but it may change the flavor a bit. I am less concerned with details like that than I am with the effects on health.)

Salt and pepper to taste

Preparation:

1. Preheat oven to 375 degrees F.

2. Cut spaghetti squash in half and clean out seeds. Place squash face down on a baking dish. Fill baking dish halfway with water. Bake for 40-45 minutes or until soft but not over-cooked. Squash is finished when fork goes in easily and shreds squash like spaghetti. Place "noodles" in a large serving dish.

3. While squash is baking, heat oil in a skillet over medium heat. Add onions and garlic, and sauté for 3 minutes.

4. Stir in ground turkey. Cook for 7-10 minutes, breaking the meat into small pieces with wooden spoon.

5. When meat is lightly browned add tomato paste and cook for 3 minutes, stirring frequently.

6. Add chopped tomatoes, vegetable broth, and mushrooms. Lower heat, cover, and simmer for 10-15 minutes.

7. Stir in soy creamer, oregano, and basil. Season with salt and pepper and cook for 1 more minute. Serve over spaghetti squash.

Nutritional information per serving:

210 calories	299 mg sodium
9 g fat	16 g carbohydrates
4 g saturated fat	3 g fiber
53 mg cholesterol	17 g protein

RELAX AND REJUVENATE: DINNERS

Crowd-Pleasing Cioppino

gf   ng

This "seafood stew" is a favorite among guests!

Ingredients:

1 pound white firm fish (sea bass, halibut, cod), cubed

1 pound large shrimp, uncooked, peeled, and deveined

1 pound clams or mussels

½ pound bay scallops

2 tablespoons coconut oil

1 onion, chopped

1 celery stalk, chopped

3 tablespoons shallots, chopped

1 pinch saffron

1 teaspoon paprika

1 bay leaf

5 garlic cloves, minced

2 ½ cups fresh diced tomatoes (or 1 16-ounce can diced tomatoes with juice in a pinch)

1 16-ounce can tomato sauce

3 cups vegetable broth

3 tablespoons parsley, chopped

Salt and pepper to taste

Preparation:

1. In a heavy-bottomed pot, heat coconut oil over medium heat. Add onion, celery, shallots, saffron, paprika, and bay leaf. Cook for 6 minutes.

2. Add garlic, and cook for 1 more minute.

3. Add tomatoes, tomato sauce, and vegetable broth. Bring it to a boil. Reduce heat and simmer for 20 minutes.

4. Add the fish, shrimp, mussels, and scallops.

5. Season with salt and pepper. Simmer for 5 minutes or until fish is cooked through and clams open. Sprinkle with parsley, and serve with a large salad and vegetable dish.

Nutritional information per serving:

327 calories	467 mg sodium
9 g fat	16 g carbohydrates
4 g saturated fat	3 g fiber
157 mg cholesterol	45 g protein

Rosemary Chicken

ng **gf**

Ingredients:

2 free-range, hormone-free, boneless, skinless chicken breasts (4-6 ounces each)

1 teaspoon fresh rosemary, chopped

1 teaspoon fresh sage, chopped

3 garlic cloves, minced

1 tablespoon grape seed oil

2 tablespoons red wine vinegar

½ teaspoon honey

¼ teaspoon salt

¼ teaspoon pepper

Preparation:

1. In a medium bowl, mix rosemary, sage, garlic, grape seed oil, vinegar, honey, salt, and pepper.

2. Add chicken and coat thoroughly. Cover and refrigerate for minimum 1 hour, up to 24 hours.

3. Preheat the grill to medium heat.

4. Remove chicken from marinade and grill for 8-10 minutes per side or until chicken is no longer pink in center. Serve with large salad or favorite greens.

Nutritional information per serving:

198 calories	656 mg sodium
8 g fat	3 g carbohydrates
1 g saturated fat	0 g fiber
66 mg cholesterol	27 g protein

RELAX AND REJUVENATE: DINNERS

Low-Cal Lo Mein with Veggies

v gf ng

This vegetarian version of the Chinese cuisine staple definitely gets the seal of approval on all levels. You'll love the way it tastes. Plus, it is loaded with good-for-you veggies and phytonutrients, and it is virtually free of refined carbohydrates. Since this is a low-calorie meal, you may indulge in a healthy snack or dessert later, guilt-free!

Ingredients:

16 ounces Shirataki noodles (see page 54 for cooking instructions).

2 tablespoons coconut oil

1 teaspoon ginger, grated

3 garlic cloves, minced

1 red onion, julienned

1 cup shiitake mushrooms, sliced

1 red bell pepper, thinly sliced

4 green onions, sliced diagonally

2 cups bean sprouts

1 cup snow peas

¼ cup water

2 tablespoons hoisin sauce (gluten-free)

1-2 tablespoons low-sodium tamari sauce

1 tablespoon arrowroot

2 tablespoons pumpkin seeds

Preparation:

1. In small bowl, mix water, tamari sauce, hoisin sauce, and arrowroot. Set aside.

2. Rinse noodles and drain. In a large pot, bring water to a boil. Add noodles and simmer for 3 minutes. Drain well.

3. Meanwhile, in a large skillet or wok, heat oil over medium heat. Add ginger and garlic, and cook for 30 seconds.

4. Stir in onion and mushrooms, and cook for 2 minutes.

5. Add red bell pepper, and cook for 1 minute.

6. Add bean sprouts and green onion last. Stir in soy sauce mixture, and cook until lightly thickened and vegetables are tender but crisp.

7. Mix in noodles, toss gently, and serve warm. Sprinkle with pumpkin seeds.

Nutritional information per serving:

204 calories	428 mg sodium
9 g fat	24 g carbohydrates
6 g saturated fat	4 g fiber
0 mg cholesterol	6 g protein

v

An excellent vegetarian dish with whole grains. To increase protein intake, consider sprinkling with raw sunflower seeds or supplementing with tofu. There is an ongoing debate about whether farro is advised for people who are gluten intolerant. My suggestion is to stay away from it if you don't eat gluten.

Ingredients:

½ cup farro grains

3 tablespoons coconut oil or grape seed oil

3 garlic cloves, minced

1 cup vegetable broth

3 cups chard, chopped

1 red onion, chopped in a large chunks

½ cup celery, chopped

1 zucchini, sliced

1 yellow squash, sliced

1 red bell pepper, diced in large chunks

1 cup Brussels sprouts, halved

1 tablespoon fresh marjoram, chopped

1 tablespoon fresh sage, chopped

1 tablespoon balsamic vinegar

¼ cup shallots, finely chopped

20 cherry tomatoes, halved

1 tablespoon fresh basil, chopped

Salt and pepper to taste

Nutritional information per serving:

268 calories	3166 mg sodium
11 g fat	38 g carbohydrates
9 g saturated fat	8 g fiber
0 mg cholesterol	9 g protein

Preparation:

1. Preheat oven to 420 degrees F.

2. In a medium, heavy-bottomed pot, heat 1 tablespoon grape seed oil over medium heat. Add garlic and cook for 2 minutes.

3. Stir in farro and vegetable broth. Bring it to a boil, then lower heat and simmer for about 30 minutes or until farro is tender. If necessary, add a little water (about ½ cup) to prevent dehydration and burning.

4. While farro is cooking, spread the onion, celery, zucchini, yellow squash, red bell pepper, and Brussels sprouts on a large cookie sheet.

5. Drizzle vegetables with 1 tablespoon oil. Roast vegetables for about 20 minutes, turning them carefully once after 10 minutes of cooking.

Preparation for Sauce:

1. Heat 1 tablespoon oil over medium heat in a skillet. Add shallots and sauté for 1 minute.

2. Add tomatoes, and sauté for another 3 minutes. Add basil. Season lightly with salt and pepper.

3. Mix chard in with farro until it is wilted. In a large bowl, toss the cooked farro, vegetables, marjoram, sage, and balsamic vinegar. Serve warm with side of shrimp if desired.

RELAX AND REJUVENATE: DINNERS

Energizing Chipotle Enchiladas

Adaptable v gf

Ingredients:

4 sprouted grain or rice tortillas

¾ cup quinoa

1 teaspoon cumin

12 ounces fresh spinach

¾ cup soy or nut cheese, grated (we prefer nut cheese)

Ingredients for Chipotle Sauce:

1 tablespoon coconut oil

2 garlic cloves, minced

1 onion, diced

1 14.5-ounce can diced tomatoes

½ cup vegetable broth

½ chipotle pepper in adobo sauce

2 tablespoons fresh oregano, chopped

Ingredients for Fresh Salsa:

4 medium tomatoes, diced

1 avocado, peeled, pitted, and diced

1 shallot, diced

2 green onions, chopped

½ jalapeno pepper, seeded and minced

1 garlic clove, minced

⅓ cup fresh cilantro, chopped

1 lime, juiced

1 tablespoon olive oil

Salt and pepper to taste

Preparation for Salsa:

In a large bowl, combine chopped tomatoes, avocado, shallots, green onions, jalapeno pepper, garlic, cilantro, lime juice, and olive oil. Season with salt and pepper. Refrigerate.

Preparation for Quinoa & Chipotle Sauce:

1. Cook quinoa according to directions on package with 1 teaspoon of cumin.

2. Meanwhile, heat coconut oil in medium saucepan over medium heat. Add onions and garlic, and sauté for 5 minutes. Stir in tomatoes, vegetable broth, chipotle pepper, and oregano. Simmer for 8-10 minutes.

3. Transfer sauce to a blender and purée. Transfer chipotle sauce back to a saucepan and set aside.

Preparation for Enchiladas:

1. Preheat oven to 350 degrees F.

2. Steam spinach for 2 minutes or until wilted. Squeeze out the water.

3. Dip tortillas into chipotle sauce (one at the time), turning to coat. Fill tortillas with ¼ quinoa and spinach.

4. Use 1 tablespoon of cheese for enchilada filling. Roll up and transfer to a casserole pan.

5. Top enchiladas with remaining sauce and sprinkle with remainder soy or nut cheese. Bake for 15-20 minutes. Serve with fresh salsa.

Nutritional information per serving:

137 calories   241 mg sodium
11 g fat   33 g carbohydrates
2 g saturated fat   10 g fiber
0 mg cholesterol   9 g protein

Sinless Spinach Lasagna

Makes 10 Servings

v

Thanks to the tofu and egg whites, this mouth-watering vegetarian delight packs a powerful protein punch.

Ingredients:

8 ounces whole-wheat lasagna noodles

10 ounces silken tofu, drained

20 ounces frozen spinach, chopped

2 tablespoons whole-wheat panko breadcrumbs

2 egg whites

4 garlic cloves, minced

3 tablespoons basil, chopped

½ teaspoon nutmeg

2 15-ounce cans tomato sauce

2 plum tomatoes, chopped

1 cup soy or nut cheese (we prefer nut cheese), shredded

Salt and pepper to taste

Preparation:

1. Preheat oven to 350 degrees F.

2. Cook pasta for 6-7 minutes (don't overcook). Carefully place in cold water to stop cooking process, and drain.

3. Thaw spinach and squeeze out excess water.

4. In a medium pot, mix tomato sauce and chopped tomatoes. Simmer on medium heat for 8 minutes.

5. In a medium bowl, mash tofu with fork.

6. Add spinach, breadcrumbs, egg white, garlic, basil, and nutmeg. Season with salt and pepper. Mix to blend well.

7. Spread small amount of tomato sauce in the dish.

8. Layer with cooked pasta, then with ⅓ tomato sauce followed by ½ spinach mixture. Sprinkle with ⅓ shredded cheese. Repeat process.

9. Finish with layer of pasta, tomatoes, and remaining cheese, and sprinkle with basil.

10. Cover with aluminum foil and bake for 40-45 minutes or until lasagna is bubbly and golden brown on the edges. Let sit 10 minutes before serving.

Nutritional information per serving:

204 calories	435 mg sodium
7 g fat	29 g carbohydrates
2 g saturated fat	3 g fiber
0 mg cholesterol	8 g protein

Baked Salmon with Roasted Leeks

ng gf

Ingredients:

2 salmon fillets (4-6 ounces each)

1 tablespoon coconut oil

4 leeks, cut in half moons (white parts only)

2 tablespoons fresh parsley, chopped

½ cup light coconut milk

1 lemon, sliced

Salt and pepper to taste

Preparation:

1. Preheat oven to 400 degrees F.

2. In a medium skillet, heat oil over medium heat. Add leeks and sauté for 5 minutes, stirring occasionally.

3. Add parsley and coconut milk. Simmer until lightly thickened.

4. Season with salt and pepper as desired. Remove from heat.

5. Line baking dish with a strip of tin foil large enough to wrap fish in. Place single layer of the lemon slices in the middle of the foil.

6. Lightly season fish with salt and pepper as desired.

7. Place salmon on top of lemon slices. Top with roasted leeks. Fold foil around fish, sealing well.

8. Bake for 12-15 minutes.

9. Transfer to a plate, top with sauce, sprinkle with parsley, and serve warm.

Nutritional information per serving:

436 calories	125 mg sodium
23 g fat	35 g carbohydrates
12 g saturated fat	6 g fiber
80 mg cholesterol	33 g protein

RELAX AND REJUVENATE: DINNERS

Ingredients:

2 boneless, skinless chicken breasts (4-6 ounces each), cut into 1-inch cubes

2 tablespoons grape seed oil

1 tablespoon honey

2 tablespoons tamari sauce or low-sodium soy sauce

1 tablespoon Dijon mustard

1 teaspoon rice vinegar

3 garlic cloves, minced

½ teaspoon pepper

2 teaspoons fresh thyme, chopped

1 red bell pepper, cut into 2-inch pieces

1 small red onion, cut into 2-inch pieces

1 zucchini, cut into 1-inch slices

10 small mushrooms

Skewers

Preparation:

1. In a large bowl, whisk together oil, honey, tamari or soy sauce, mustard, rice vinegar, garlic, pepper, and thyme.

2. Add chicken, bell peppers, onions, zucchini, and mushrooms. Toss to coat and refrigerate for up to 24 hours.

3. Preheat the grill to high heat.

4. Thread chicken and vegetables alternately onto skewers.

5. Lightly oil the grill. Place skewers on grill and cook, turning frequently for about 15-20 minutes, until chicken is cooked through and vegetables are tender.

Nutritional information per serving:

290 calories	669 mg sodium
15 g fat	10 g carbohydrates
2 g saturated fat	1 g fiber
66 mg cholesterol	29 g protein

RELAX AND REJUVENATE: DINNERS

Snapper with Tomato Caper Sauce

Makes 2 Servings

gf · ng

Ingredients:

2 snapper fillets (4-6 ounces each)

1 tablespoon grape seed oil

1 shallot, chopped

1 garlic clove, minced

1 anchovy fillet

1 bay leaf

1 tablespoon tomato paste

¼ cup vegetable broth

1 tablespoon capers

1 Roma tomato, diced

¼ cup soy creamer or coconut creamer (coconut creamer may give a different flavor)

1 teaspoon fresh lemon juice

Salt and pepper to taste

Preparation:

1. Preheat oven to 400 degrees F.

2. Brush snapper with oil and sprinkle with salt and pepper.

3. Arrange in baking dish and bake for 20 minutes or until fish flakes easily with a fork.

4. Meanwhile, heat the rest of the grape seed oil over medium heat. Sauté shallots, garlic, anchovy, and bay leaf for 2 minutes.

5. Stir in tomato paste, and cook for 2 more minutes.

6. Add vegetable broth and deglaze the pan.

7. Stir in capers and tomatoes, and cook for 3 minutes.

8. Add soy creamer. Season with salt and pepper to taste.

9. Simmer until lightly thickened.

10. Add lemon juice. Serve baked snapper with tomato caper sauce.

Nutritional information per serving:

297 calories	284 mg sodium
11 g fat	15 g carbohydrates
1 g saturated fat	1 g fiber
55 mg cholesterol	33 g protein

Lentil Pilaf

gf ng v

Lentils are high in fiber and a good source of protein for vegetarians and vegans. Because they are so high in fiber, they are very filling and will keep you feeling satiated for hours.

Ingredients for Pilaf:

1 tablespoon coconut

2 leeks, sliced into half moons (white part only)

3 garlic cloves, minced

1 cup red bell pepper, chopped

1 cup red lentils (Always soak overnight and cook thoroughly.)

2 teaspoons fresh thyme

½ teaspoon cumin

1 teaspoon fresh lemon juice

3 cups vegetable broth

Salt and pepper to taste

Ingredients for Cilantro Dressing:

½ cup cilantro, chopped

1 garlic clove, minced

1 tablespoon lemon juice

1 tablespoon tahini paste

2 tablespoons water

Salt to taste

Preparation for Dressing:

1. In a small food processor, place cilantro, garlic, lemon juice, and tahini. Blend into a coarse paste.

2. Add water to the paste, and blend until smooth and creamy. Season with salt. Set aside.

Preparation for Pilaf:

1. In a large pot, heat oil over medium heat. Add leeks and garlic and sauté for 2 minutes.

2. Add bell pepper and cook for 2 more minutes.

3. Stir in lentils, thyme, cumin, lemon juice, and vegetable broth. Season with salt and pepper if desired.

4. Bring to a boil, then reduce the heat and simmer for about 15-20 minutes or until lentils are tender and liquid is absorbed. Serve topped with cilantro dressing.

Nutritional information per serving:

165 calories	121 mg sodium
6 g fat	23 g carbohydrates
3 g saturated fat	7 g fiber
0 mg cholesterol	6 g protein

Pilaf only nutritional information:

140 calories	117 mg sodium
4 g fat	22 g carbohydrates
3 g saturated fat	6 g fiber
0 mg cholesterol	6 g protein

ng **gf** **Adaptable**

If you are gluten sensitive, omit the flour. It helps to thicken the sauce. Your sauce will be thin, but the flavor will be the same. I am far less concerned with details like the consistency of the sauce than I am with feeling great.

Ingredients:

2 free-range, hormone-free chicken breasts (4-6 ounces each), thinly sliced

4 garlic cloves, minced

1 tablespoon whole-wheat flour (rice flour for gluten-free)

2 tablespoons coconut oil

2 cups crimini mushrooms, sliced

½ cup vegetable stock

½ cup Marsala wine

2 tablespoons Italian parsley, chopped

1 tablespoon fresh thyme, chopped

½ teaspoon paprika

Salt and pepper to taste

Preparation:

1. Season chicken with salt, pepper, and paprika. Spread garlic over meat.

2. Add flour to a plate. Dredge chicken in flour, shaking to remove any excess flour.

3. In a skillet, heat oil over medium-high heat. Cook chicken about 3 minutes on each side, remove from skillet and keep warm.

4. Add mushrooms to skillet, and cook for 4 minutes, stirring frequently. Add broth and wine to skillet. Bring to a boil, and cook until slightly thickened, about 5 minutes. Lower the heat to medium and return chicken to skillet, heat it through. Add parsley and thyme, and mix. Serve with green salad, quinoa, or brown rice.

Nutritional information per serving:

377 calories	495 mg sodium
15 g fat	17 g carbohydrates
12 g saturated fat	2 g fiber
66 mg cholesterol	30 g protein

RELAX AND REJUVENATE: DINNERS

"Spaghetti" with Turkey Meatballs

Makes 4 Servings

gf · ng

Another guilt-free meal! Indulge and enjoy!

Ingredients:

1 pound free-range, antibiotic-free ground turkey

3 green onions, chopped

2 garlic cloves, minced

¼ cup parsley, chopped

¾ cup celery, finely chopped

½ teaspoon garlic salt

1 28-ounce can diced tomatoes, low-sodium (or use 4-5 cups fresh diced tomatoes to reduce sodium)

½-1 chipotle pepper in adobo sauce (as desired for spicy flavor)

1 onion, chopped

16 ounces Shirataki noodles

½ cup soy creamer or coconut creamer

2 tablespoons fresh basil, chopped

Preparation:

1. In a large bowl, mix turkey, green onion, garlic, parsley, celery, and garlic salt. Shape into 1-inch meatballs and place onto tray.

2. Heat oil in skillet over medium heat. Add meatballs to pan, browning on all sides, about 5-10 minutes.

3. Meanwhile, make the tomato sauce. Place tomatoes, chipotle pepper, and onion in a blender bowl. Blend until smooth.

4. Add to browned meatballs, and simmer for 30 minutes.

5. About 5 minutes before meatballs are finished simmering, boil water in a pot. Empty and drain Shirataki noodles from package. You may want to cut noodles before boiling. Add to boiling water. Reduce heat and simmer for 3 minutes. Drain the noodles well (they tend to hold water).

6. When meatballs are finished cooking, add creamer and simmer for 2 more minutes. Stir in basil. Serve over Shirataki noodles and with favorite greens.

Nutritional information per serving:

260 calories	558 mg sodium
10 g fat	17 g carbohydrates
3 g saturated fat	3 g fiber
80 mg cholesterol	25 g protein

RELAX AND REJUVENATE: DINNERS

112

Tempting Tomato Pizza

v

When your kids are screaming for pizza, don't pick up the phone and order a greasy pie from the local pizza parlor. Try this quick and much healthier version. We make it for kids' parties, and they love it.

Ingredients:

16 ounces ready whole-wheat pizza dough

10 Roma tomatoes, blanched, deseeded, and sliced

3 tablespoons basil pesto

½ cup soy cheese or nut cheese, shredded

1 tablespoon fresh basil, chopped

1 tablespoon fresh oregano, chopped

¼ cup olive oil

1 tablespoon fresh lemon juice

1 teaspoon honey (agave or rice syrup for vegans)

1 garlic clove, minced

½ teaspoon garlic salt

Preparation:

1. To blanch tomatoes, use a sharp paring knife to remove the stem core. Place in a large bowl and pour enough boiling water to cover them. After 3 minutes, plunge tomatoes into a large bowl of ice-cold water. Remove tomatoes from water and remove their skins. Cut tomatoes in half, remove the seeds, and slice them. Set aside.

2. Preheat the oven to 450 degrees F.

3. Place dough in the middle of a baking sheet. Use your fingertips to flatten and stretch it out to the edges of the baking sheet. Let it rest at room temperature for 30 minutes.

4. Spread pesto evenly over pizza dough.

5. Sprinkle with 2 tablespoons of cheese, then arrange tomato slices in a single layer.

6. Top with remaining cheese.

7. Bake 10-20 minutes or until golden brown.

8. While pizza is baking, mix olive oil, lemon juice, honey, garlic, and garlic salt in a small bowl. Set aside.

9. Garnish hot pizza with fresh basil and oregano. Drizzle with dressing. Serve immediately.

Nutritional information per serving:

299 calories	471 mg sodium
16 g fat	35 g carbohydrates
3 g saturated fat	3 g fiber
1 mg cholesterol	6 g protein

Easy Eggplant Parmesan

Makes 6 Servings

We've modified this classic vegetarian dish to boost the nutritional value and reduce the calories.

Ingredients:

3 medium eggplants, peeled and sliced into ¼-inch rounds (Always cook eggplant thoroughly to reduce the effect of lectins.)

4 egg whites, beaten

2 cups whole-wheat panko breadcrumbs

2 14.5-ounce cans low-sodium tomato sauce

6 plum tomatoes, chopped

½ teaspoon garlic salt

¾ cup vegetarian cheese, shredded (we prefer nut cheese)

2 tablespoons fresh basil, chopped

Salt and pepper to taste

Preparation:

1. Preheat oven to 350 degrees F.

2. In a medium pot over medium heat, mix tomato sauce, chopped tomatoes, and garlic salt. Bring to a boil. Reduce heat and simmer for 10 minutes.

3. Season eggplant with salt and pepper as desired.

4. Dip eggplant slices in egg whites, then dredge in breadcrumbs.

5. Arrange in a single layer on a cookie sheet and bake for 15 minutes. Turn over and bake for 15 more minutes on other side.

6. In a 9 x 12-inch baking dish, spread ⅓ of tomato sauce. Spread ½ of baked eggplant on the cookie sheet. Spread eggplant with ⅓ of tomato sauce. Sprinkle with ½ of shredded cheese. Repeat layering process. Top with layer of tomato sauce and remaining cheese and sprinkle with basil.

7. Cover with aluminum foil and bake for 30-35 minutes or until golden brown.

Nutritional information per serving:

287 calories	354 mg sodium
7 g fat	47 g carbohydrates
2 g saturated fat	11 g fiber
0 mg cholesterol	11 g protein

RELAX AND REJUVENATE: DINNERS

ng **gf**

Moussaka is one of my all-time favorite dishes. We have modified the traditional recipe to reduce the calories and pump up the nutritional value, and everyone who tries it loves it. No one seems to miss the excess fat, salt, and refined carbohydrates.

Ingredients:

3 medium eggplants, sliced into ¼-inch rounds (Always cook eggplant thoroughly to reduce the effect of lectins.)

3 large zucchini, cut lengthwise into ¼-inch slices

2 tablespoons grape seed oil

1½ pounds lean, grass-fed, hormone-free ground beef or lamb

1 tablespoon coconut oil

2 onions, diced

6 garlic cloves, minced

½ teaspoon ground cinnamon

½ teaspoon ground allspice

3 cups fresh tomatoes, diced (or use 1 14-ounce can of low-sodium tomatoes with juice, but this increases the sodium substantially)

1 tablespoon tomato paste

1 teaspoon garlic salt

⅓ cup fresh parsley, chopped

1 cup vegetarian cheese, grated (we prefer nut cheese)

Salt and pepper to taste

Nutritional information per serving:

442 calories	261 mg sodium
33 g fat	22 g carbohydrates
13 g saturated fat	6 g fiber
62 mg cholesterol	17 g protein

Preparation:

1. Preheat grill to medium-high and preheat oven to 375 degrees F.

2. Brush eggplant and zucchini lightly with grape seed oil.

3. Grill vegetables until tender and golden brown.

4. Meanwhile, heat 1 tablespoon coconut oil in large skillet over medium-high heat. Add onion and cook for 4 minutes.

5. Stir in garlic and meat, and cook for 10-15 minutes or until meat is no longer pink. Stir meat frequently, breaking it into small pieces.

6. Add cinnamon, allspice, tomatoes, tomato paste, and garlic salt. Lower the heat and simmer for 10 minutes.

7. Stir in parsley and season with salt and pepper. Set aside.

8. In a 9 x 12-inch baking dish, arrange ⅓ of the eggplant slices. Sprinkle with 2 tablespoons panko breadcrumbs (optional), followed by ½ of the zucchini.

9. Spread ½ of the meat and sprinkle with ⅓ of the cheese.

10. Repeat layering of eggplant, breadcrumbs, zucchini, meat, and cheese.

11. Finish top layer with eggplant, and sprinkle with remainder of the cheese.

12. Cover with aluminum foil. Bake moussaka until golden brown, about 40 minutes. Remove from oven and let rest for 10 minutes. Use spatula to serve.

RELAX AND REJUVENATE: DINNERS

Grilled Polenta with Roasted Beans

gf v

We have a bit of a "polenta war" going on in the Amen household. Daniel loves traditional polenta, which is made with cornmeal. I prefer making an amazing chestnut polenta that has a delightful nutty flavor. I decided to give you both versions here so you can make them both and have a taste test in your own home to see which one you and your family prefer.

Ingredients for Polenta:

1 pound prepared polenta, sliced into ¾-inch thick rounds (see page 121 for Chestnut Polenta ingredients and preparation)

Ingredients for Roasted Beans:

½ cup shallots, diced

3 garlic cloves, minced

2 cups green beans

2 cups yellow beans

1 cup organic edamame

1 teaspoon garlic salt

1 tablespoon basil, chopped

1 tablespoon thyme, chopped

1 tablespoon parsley, chopped

Pepper to taste

Ingredients for Tomato Sauce:

1 tablespoon coconut oil

⅓ cup shallots, diced

1½ cup cherry tomatoes, halved

1 tablespoon basil, chopped

1 tablespoon parsley, chopped

1 tablespoon fresh lemon juice

1 tablespoon olive oil

Salt and pepper to taste

Preparation:

1. Preheat the grill to medium-high heat.

2. Brush polenta with grape seed oil on both sides and grill for 4-5 minutes or until golden brown, turning once.

3. In a large skille, heat oil over medium heat. Add shallots and sauté for 1 minute.

4. Add green beans. Sauté for 4 minutes, adding a little water if necessary and stirring frequently.

5. Add yellow beans and cook for 3 minutes.

6. Add edamame and cook for 1 more minute.

7. Stir in garlic salt, basil, thyme, and parsley. Season with pepper as desired. Keep warm.

Preparation for Tomato Sauce:

1. In a medium skillet, heat oil over medium heat. Add shallots and cook for 1 minute.

2. Add tomatoes. Sauté for 3 minutes.

3. Stir in basil, parsley, and lemon juice. Season with salt and pepper as desired. Remove from heat and swirl in olive oil.

4. Place roasted beans on a platter.

5. Place grilled polenta over beans and top with tomato sauce.

Nutritional information per serving:

250 calories

7 g fat

2 g saturated fat

0 mg cholesterol

233 mg sodium

27 g carbohydrates

9 g fiber

8 g protein

Polenta only nutritional information:

40 calories

0 g fat

0 g saturated fat

0 mg cholesterol

148 mg sodium

9 g carbohydrates

1 g fiber

1 g protein

v   gf

This chestnut polenta recipe is a great alternative to traditional cornmeal polenta. You can prepare it for the Grilled Polenta with Roasted Beans recipe found on page 118 or with many of the sauces found in this cookbook. You can also use it as a vegan option for dishes that are prepared with meat.

Ingredients

4 cups water

1 pound chestnut flour

¼ teaspoon sea salt

Preparation for Chestnut Polenta:

1. Boil water in a large pot with salt.

2. Add flour slowly until water and flour level are even.

3. Cook for 10 minutes or until all water is completely absorbed. Do not stir during this time.

4. Cook for an additional 5 minutes, stirring continuously, until mixture takes on the "grainy-like" texture of polenta. As it thickens it will begin to resemble porridge.

5. Break apart lumps and stir mixture until smooth and thick.

6. Let cool until you are able to handle. You can form polenta into ¾-inch rounds and allow them to cool and set.

7. Follow the cooking instructions on page 118 but note that when grilling homemade polenta rounds, you may want to use a grilling rack to prevent crumbling. They may not hold together as well as prepared cornmeal polenta.

Nutritional information per serving:

186 calories	42 mg sodium
2 g fat	39 g carbohydrates
0 g saturated fat	5 g fiber
0 mg cholesterol	3 g protein

RELAX AND REJUVENATE: DINNERS

Lemon Pepper Halibut

gf ng

Ingredients:

4 halibut fillets (4-6 ounces each)

1 tablespoon olive oil

2 tablespoons grape seed oil

4 cups arugula

½ cup sun-dried tomatoes

3 garlic cloves

¼ cup basil

¼ cup red wine vinegar

2 tablespoons water

Lemon pepper to taste

Salt to taste

Preparation:

1. Preheat oven to 400 degrees F.

2. Place sun-dried tomatoes, garlic, and basil in a blender. Blend until smooth.

3. For sun-dried tomato dressing, add water and 1 tablespoon of olive oil to blender, add water and pulse a few times, until well mixed. Season with salt as desired. Set aside.

4. Lightly brush halibut with grape seed oil and sprinkle with lemon pepper and salt.

5. Transfer to a baking dish and bake for 20-30 minutes or until fish flakes easily when tested with a fork.

6. Place fillets on a bed of arugula and top with sun-dried tomato dressing.

Nutritional information per serving:

274 calories	226 mg sodium
14 g fat	5 g carbohydrates
2 g saturated fat	1 g fiber
46 mg cholesterol	32 g protein

Hawaiian Blackened Tuna with Mango Salsa

What can I say? Incredibly simple and unbelievably delicious!

Ingredients:

2 wild ahi tuna steaks (4-6 ounces each)

Head of red or green endive

1 tablespoon grape seed oil

1 tablespoon fresh lime juice

1 tablespoon fresh marjoram, chopped

1 tablespoon fresh cilantro, chopped

½ teaspoon ground mustard powder

½ teaspoon chili powder

½ teaspoon garlic powder

½ teaspoon paprika

Optional: ½ teaspoon salt

Ingredients for Mango Salsa:

1 tablespoon grape seed oil

1 tablespoon fresh lime juice

1 tablespoon cilantro, chopped

1 mango, peeled, pitted, and diced

½ red bell pepper, finely chopped

1 tablespoon shallots, finely chopped

1 tablespoon chives, finely chopped

Salt and pepper as desired

Optional: ½ jalapeno, seeded and minced

Preparation:

1. For tuna herb mixture, mix grape seed oil, lime juice, marjoram, cilantro, mustard powder, chili powder, garlic powder, paprika, and salt in a small bowl.

2. Brush each tuna steak with herb mixture, patting into fish with fingertips. Cover and refrigerate for 1 hour.

3. For mango salsa, mix grape seed oil, lime juice, and cilantro in a medium bowl.

4. Stir in mango, bell peppers, shallots, chives, and jalapeno (if desired). Season with salt and pepper. Set aside.

5. Heat a medium skillet over medium heat. You should not need extra oil for cooking because the fish was marinated in oil. Place tuna steaks in pan and sear, about 1-2 minutes per side depending on how cooked you prefer them. Don't overcook, it should be pink on the inside. Transfer tuna to a cutting board and slice against the grain.

6. Arrange the endive leaves on a platter and top with mango salsa. Place sliced tuna on the side.

Nutritional information per serving:

421 calories	121 mg sodium
16 g fat	34 g carbohydrates
2 g saturated fat	11 g fiber
66 mg cholesterol	39 g protein

Tuna only nutritional information:

233 calories	61 mg sodium
9 g fat	3 g carbohydrates
1 g saturated fat	1 g fiber
66 mg cholesterol	35 g protein

RELAX AND REJUVENATE: DINNERS

Shirataki Noodles with Edamame and Smoked Salmon

gf ng

Ingredients:

16 ounces Shirataki noodles

6 ounces wild smoked salmon, torn into bite-sized pieces

¼ cup Vegenaise®

2 tablespoons fresh lemon juice

1 cup organic edamame, shelled

4 green onions, chopped

1 tablespoon parsley, chopped

1 tablespoon mint, chopped

Coarse black pepper to taste

Preparation:

1. In a large bowl, mix salmon, Vegenaise®, lemon juice, edamame, and green onions. Set aside.

2. Bring water to a boil in a medium pot. Empty and drain Shirataki noodles from package. You may want to cut noodles before boiling. Add to boiling water. Reduce heat and simmer for 3 minutes.

3. Drain the noodles well (they tend to retain water).

4. Add salmon mixture to noodles.

5. Gently toss parsley and mint with salmon and noodles. Season with pepper. Serve with a large salad.

Nutritional information per serving:

482 calories	250 mg sodium
29 g fat	17 g carbohydrates
4 g saturated fat	4 g fiber
60 mg cholesterol	32 g protein

Tempeh with Vegetables

Makes 2 Servings

gf ng v

Ingredients:

8 ounces tempeh, diced into cubes (soy tempeh)

2 tablespoons low-sodium tamari sauce

1 tablespoon apple cider vinegar

3 garlic cloves, minced

2 tablespoons coconut oil

3 shallots, sliced

1 cup crimini mushrooms, sliced

8 ounces broccolini

1 red bell pepper, sliced

4 green onions, sliced

Preparation:

1. In a medium bowl, mix tamari sauce, apple cider vinegar, and garlic.

2. Coat tempeh with marinade, cover, and refrigerate for 1 hour.

3. In a large skillet, heat oil over medium heat. Add shallots and sauté for 1 minute.

4. Add mushrooms and cook for 2 minutes.

5. Add broccolini and bell pepper and sauté for 2 more minutes.

6. Add the tempeh with the marinade and cook 5 minutes. Serve over favorite greens or rice noodles.

Nutritional information per serving:

344 calories	1028 mg sodium
23 g fat	20 g carbohydrates
14 g saturated fat	3 g fiber
0 mg cholesterol	21 g protein

SOOTHE YOUR SOUL: SOUPS

Chapter 6

SOOTHE YOUR SOUL: SOUPS

Chapter 6

Soups are a favorite in the Amen household. They are easy to prepare and you can add so many wonderful vegetables and herbs. But the best part about soups is that they are a comfort food. Plus, you can prepare them in advance and serve them the following day (actually, soups are one of the few dishes that often taste better that way). Remember not to overcook your veggies when making soups.

SOOTHE YOUR SOUL: SOUPS

Healing Chicken Vegetable Soup

Makes 6 Servings

This is a perfectly satisfying meal for a rainy day... or any day for that matter!

Ingredients:

2 tablespoons coconut oil

1 bay leaf

2 celery stalks, sliced

2 leeks, cut in half moons (white parts only)

1 carrot, peeled and diced

1 parsnip, peeled and diced

2 boneless, skinless chicken breasts (4-6 ounces each), cut in cubes

1 cup water

5 cups vegetable broth

1½ cup green cabbage, shredded

2 tablespoons fresh parsley, chopped

Salt and pepper to taste

Preparation:

1. In a large pot, heat oil over medium-high heat. Add bay leaf, celery, leeks, carrot, and parsnip, and sauté for 2-3 minutes, stirring frequently.

2. Add chicken and cook for 4 more minutes.

3. Stir in water and vegetable broth. Bring it to a boil, reduce heat, and simmer for 15-20 minutes.

4. Add cabbage, and simmer for 5 minutes. Season with salt and pepper as desired.

5. Top with parsley and serve hot.

Nutritional information per serving:

188 calories	199 mg sodium
6 g fat	14 g carbohydrates
4 g saturated fat	3 g fiber
46 mg cholesterol	20 g protein

Mindful Minestrone Soup

IIIIIIIIIIIIIIIIIIIIIIIIIIIIIIIIIIIIIIIIIIIIIIIIIIIIIIIIIIIIIIIIIIIIIIIIIIIIIIIIIIIIIIIIII

Makes 6 Servings

Adaptable   v   gf   ng

Minestrone soup is a favorite in the Amen household. Our version is filled with nutrient-rich veggies and high-fiber beans that keep you feeling full longer. If you love pasta in your minestrone soup, try adding Shirataki orzo-style noodles.

Ingredients:

¼ cup vegetable broth or 2 tablespoons coconut oil (we prefer broth)

1 onion, coarsely chopped

2 celery stalks, chopped

2 small potatoes, cubed

1 carrot, chopped

1 zucchini, sliced

1 teaspoon fresh thyme

1 bay leaf

1 15-ounce can stewed tomatoes

4 cups low-sodium vegetable broth

2 cups kidney beans, soaked, rinsed, and cooked (only use canned beans in a pinch)

2 cups fresh spinach

2 tablespoons fresh parsley

Salt and pepper to taste

Optional: Shirataki orzo-style noodles (See page 54 for cooking instructions.)

Preparation:

1. Heat ¼ cup vegetable broth for sautéing, or coconut oil if desired. Stir in onion, celery, potatoes, and carrot. Stir frequently for about 5 minutes.

2. Add zucchini, thyme, and bay leaf, and cook for another 2 minutes.

3. Stir in tomatoes and vegetable broth. Bring to a boil, reduce heat, and simmer for 10 minutes. Stir in beans and pasta (if desired), and simmer for 10 minutes.

4. Add spinach and parsley last, just before serving. Stir in and let settle for a minute. Season with salt and pepper to taste.

Nutritional information per serving:

173 calories	573 mg sodium
1 g fat	36 g carbohydrates
0 g saturated fat	9 g fiber
0 mg cholesterol	7 g protein

SOOTHE YOUR SOUL: SOUPS

134

Heavenly Herbed Split Pea and Sweet Potato Soup

v   gf

Ingredients:

2 tablespoons vegetable broth

1 onion, chopped

3 celery stalks, sliced

2 garlic cloves, minced

4 cups water

6 cups low-sodium vegetable broth

2 cups dried split peas

¼ cup barley

3 sweet potatoes, diced

1 tablespoon fresh rosemary, chopped

1 tablespoon fresh thyme, chopped

1 tablespoon fresh marjoram, chopped

1 teaspoon cumin

½ teaspoon curry

1 teaspoon garlic salt

½ teaspoon lemon pepper

Salt and pepper to taste

Preparation:

1. Heat 1-2 tablespoons vegetable broth in a large pot over medium heat. Add onions, celery, and garlic, and sauté for 2-3 minutes.

2. Add remaining vegetable broth, water, peas, and barley. Bring to a boil, then reduce heat to low, and simmer for 40 minutes.

3. Add sweet potatoes and herbs. Simmer for another 30-40 minutes or until peas and potatoes are tender.

4. Add salt and pepper to taste. Ladle into soup bowls and serve hot.

Nutritional information per serving:

188 calories	344 mg sodium
1 g fat	38 g carbohydrates
0 g saturated fat	11 g fiber
0 mg cholesterol	8 g protein

So-Good Miso Soup

Makes 4 Servings

Ingredients:

4 cups low-sodium vegetable broth

3 tablespoons light miso paste

8 ounces firm tofu, drained and diced

1 cup shiitake mushrooms, sliced

4 green onions, thinly sliced

1 cup baby spinach

1 teaspoon tamari sauce

1 teaspoon rice vinegar

Preparation:

1. In a medium pot, bring water to a boil. Whisk in miso paste and lower heat.

2. Add tofu, mushrooms, green onions, baby spinach, tamari sauce, and rice vinegar. Simmer for 2 minutes. Serve warm.

Nutritional information per serving:

74 calories

2 g fat

0 g saturated fat

0 mg cholesterol

263 mg sodium

11 g carbohydrates

2 g fiber

4 g protein

SOOTHE YOUR SOUL: SOUPS

137

White Bean Soup for the Wise

Makes 6 Servings

This soup is the perfect combination of textures. It's got just enough flavor to be really interesting.

Ingredients:

1 pound dried white lima beans

2 tablespoons coconut oil

1 onion, chopped

4 celery stalks, sliced

2 leeks, cut in half moons (white parts only)

4 garlic cloves, minced

1 bay leaf

1 teaspoon garlic salt

½ teaspoon curry

⅛ teaspoon nutmeg

⅛ teaspoon cinnamon

2 teaspoons cumin

1 teaspoon fresh rosemary, chopped

1 teaspoon fresh thyme, chopped

1 teaspoon fresh marjoram, chopped

6 cups vegetable broth

3 cups water

1 pound kale, stems discarded and leaves chopped

Salt and pepper to taste

Preparation:

1. In a large bowl, cover beans with cold water and soak overnight.

2. Drain and rinse well.

3. In a large pot, heat oil over medium heat. Add onion and celery, and sauté for 5 minutes.

4. Add garlic, bay leaf, garlic salt, curry, nutmeg, cinnamon, and cumin, and cook for 1 more minute.

5. Add beans, rosemary, thyme, marjoram, vegetable broth, and water. Cover, bring to a boil, reduce heat, and simmer for 40-50 minutes, stirring occasionally.

6. Stir in kale and simmer for 15 minutes. Season with salt and pepper as desired.

Nutritional information per serving:

207 calories	351 mg sodium
6 g fat	33 g carbohydrates
4 g saturated fat	10 g fiber
0 mg cholesterol	7 g protein

SOOTHE YOUR SOUL: SOUPS

Brain-Friendly Black Bean Bisque

Makes 6 Servings

v   gf   ng

Ingredients:

1 pound dry black beans

1 tablespoon coconut oil

2 onions, chopped

2 celery stalks, sliced

1 carrot, peeled and diced

3 garlic cloves, minced

1 bay leaf

2 teaspoons ground cumin

2 teaspoons fresh oregano, chopped

½-1 chipotle pepper in adobo sauce

6 cups vegetable broth

Salt and pepper to taste

Cilantro for garnish

Preparation:

1. In a large bowl, cover beans with cold water and soak overnight.

2. Drain and rinse well.

3. In a large pot, heat oil over medium heat. Add onion, celery, and carrot, and sauté for 5 minutes.

4. Add garlic, bay leaf, cumin, oregano, and chipotle pepper. Cook for 1 more minute.

5. Add beans and vegetable broth. Bring it a boil. Reduce heat, cover, and simmer for 1½ hours or until beans are tender. Season with salt and pepper as desired.

6. Remove from heat. Remove the bay leaf and purée soup using an immersion blender. Garnish with cilantro and serve hot.

Nutritional information per serving:

164 calories	233 mg sodium
3 g fat	27 g carbohydrates
2 g saturated fat	9 g fiber
0 mg cholesterol	8 g protein

Creamy Broccoli Soup

Ingredients:

1 pound broccoli

1 tablespoon coconut oil

1 small onion, chopped

1 leek, chopped (white parts only)

⅓ cup celery, chopped

1 tablespoon whole-wheat flour (leave this out if you are gluten sensitive)

3 cups vegetable stock

¼ cup soy creamer

Salt and pepper to taste

Preparation:

1. Cut woodsy ends from broccoli, peel, and chop. Reserve ½ cup broccoli florets (very small) for garnish.

2. In a medium-sized stockpot, heat oil over medium heat. Add onion, leeks, and celery. Sauté for 5 minutes.

3. Add the broccoli, and cook for another 2 minutes.

4. Add flour, and stir well to combine. Stir frequently, and cook for 3-4 minutes. Reduce heat to low. Mix in 1 cup of vegetable stock and whisk to work out any lumps.

5. Purée vegetables in blender and transfer back to the pot.

6. Add remaining vegetable stock and soy creamer. Bring it to a boil, lower the heat, cover and simmer for 5-10 minutes or until thickened. Season with salt and pepper. Sprinkle with reserved broccoli florets and serve.

Nutritional information per serving:

77 calories	106 mg sodium
3 g fat	10 g carbohydrates
2 g saturated fat	4 g fiber
0 mg cholesterol	3 g protein

Slim and Sleek Roasted Tomato Soup

Makes 6 Servings

gf   v

Once you've had this succulent tomato soup, you'll never go back to canned! Roasting the tomatoes enhances their natural flavor and also reduces the effect of lectins that raw tomatoes contain.

Ingredients:

4 tomatoes, cut in half lengthwise

1 tablespoon grape seed oil

1 tablespoon coconut oil

2 leeks, chopped in half moons (white parts only)

⅓ cup brown rice

3 cups vegetable broth

4 cups fresh diced tomatoes (or 1 28-ounce can diced tomatoes)

2 tablespoons tomato paste

¼ cup soy creamer

½ cup almond milk

1 teaspoon sugar

1 teaspoon garlic salt

½ cup fresh basil, chopped

1 tablespoon fresh parsley, chopped

Pepper to taste

Preparation:

1. Preheat the oven to 400 degrees F.

2. Place tomatoes on a baking sheet, drizzle with grape seed oil, and roast for 45 minutes.

3. In a large pot, heat coconut oil over medium heat. Add leeks and cook for 3 minutes.

4. Add brown rice and vegetable broth. Bring it to a boil, reduce heat, cover, and simmer for 30 minutes.

5. Place roasted tomatoes, canned tomatoes, and tomato paste in a blender bowl and purée until smooth. Add to brown rice and broth, and cook another 20 minutes.

6. Add soy creamer, almond milk, sugar, garlic salt, basil, and parsley. Season with pepper as desired, and serve hot.

Nutritional information per serving:

147 calories	428 mg sodium
7 g fat	19 g carbohydrates
2 g saturated fat	3 g fiber
0 mg cholesterol	3 g protein

LIVE AND SATISFYING: SALADS

Chapter 7

LIVE AND SATISFYING: SALADS

Chapter 7

I often say to eat like a gorilla. Salads are the foods that most closely match the diet of a gorilla—lots of raw veggies, a little fruit, and some nuts and seeds. I suggest adding a large salad as a side dish to almost every recipe in this cookbook. I often eat a salad with raw or lightly cooked veggies for breakfast. That's how serious I am about this principle! Salads and smoothies are my favorites because of the amount of delicious "raw" live foods they contain. In the Amen household we add at least one cooked meal each day, but we always eat it with a big salad and another vegetable dish. Adding a little protein to your favorite salad will make it a complete meal.

Brain-Boosting BBQ Chicken Salad

Ingredients:

2 free-range, hormone-free, boneless, skinless chicken breasts (4 ounces each)

1 lime, juiced

¼ cup fresh orange juice

3 garlic cloves, minced

½ teaspoon onion powder

1 tablespoon fresh sage, chopped

1 tablespoon fresh thyme, chopped

½ teaspoon salt and pepper

1 red bell pepper, chopped

⅓ cup celery, chopped

1 cup black beans, drained and rinsed (Always soak overnight and cook thoroughly. Only use canned beans in a pinch.)

1 avocado, cut into chunks

3 green onions, chopped

4 cups mixed greens

1 tablespoon olive oil

2 tablespoons fresh lime juice

1 tablespoon cilantro, chopped

Salt and pepper to taste

Optional: 2 corn cobs (they taste great, but corn should be eaten only on occasion)

Preparation:

1. In a small bowl, combine lime and orange juice, garlic, onion powder, sage, thyme, salt, and pepper.

2. Transfer to a plastic bag. Add chicken, turn to coat, and refrigerate for 3-24 hours.

3. Preheat the grill to medium-high heat.

4. Grill the chicken for about 5-7 minutes on each side or until turkey is no longer pink in center.

5. While the meat is grilling, cook the corn (if desired). Cut the kernels off the cob and place in a small bowl. Set aside.

6. In a large bowl, mix olive oil, lime juice, and cilantro.

7. Add red bell pepper, celery, black beans, avocado, corn, and green onions. Season with salt and pepper.

8. To serve, place greens on plate and top with bean salad and slices of grilled turkey tenderloin.

Nutritional information per serving:

296 calories	332 mg sodium
14 g fat	24 g carbohydrates
2 g saturated fat	11 g fiber
21 mg cholesterol	16 g protein

Arugula Salad with Raspberries and Hemp Seeds

v gf ng

Ingredients:

8 cups arugula leaves

2 cups fresh raspberries

2 tablespoons hemp seed oil

2 tablespoons grape seed oil

1 tablespoon balsamic vinegar

1 teaspoon Dijon mustard

¼ cup hemp seeds

Salt and pepper to taste

Preparation:

1. In a small bowl, mix all oil, balsamic vinegar, and Dijon mustard.

2. Season with salt and pepper as desired. Refrigerate dressing until salad is ready to serve.

3. Place arugula on plate, top with raspberries, and sprinkle with hemp seeds. Drizzle with balsamic vinaigrette and serve.

Nutritional information per serving:

283 calories	49 mg sodium
19 g fat	14 g carbohydrates
2 g saturated fat	4 g fiber
0 mg cholesterol	15 g protein

Peaceful Asian Pear Salad

ng   gf   v

Ingredients:

8 cups arugula

1 Asian pear, cored and thinly sliced

¼ cup pecans

¼ cup grape seed oil

1 teaspoon honey (agave or rice syrup for vegans)

½ teaspoon Dijon mustard

1 tablespoon apple cider vinegar

Salt and pepper to taste

Preparation:

1. In a small bowl, combine the grape seed oil, honey, mustard, and vinegar.

2. Season with salt and pepper, then set aside.

3. On a large plate, arrange arugula and top with pear and pecans.

4. Drizzle the dressing over the salad when ready to eat.

Nutritional information per serving:

201 calories	26 mg sodium
19 g fat	7 g carbohydrates
2 g saturated fat	2 g fiber
0 mg cholesterol	2 g protein

Get Fit Fennel and Orange Salad

Makes 4 Servings

v gf ng

I typically advise people to avoid drinking fruit juice because it is so high in sugar, but the very small amount of juice used to flavor the dressing in this recipe adds very little sugar. It is preferable to consume a tiny amount of fresh juice in a salad dressing than to have the refined sugar that is used in so many processed dressings.

Ingredients:

2 fennel bulbs, cut in half and thinly sliced

3 oranges, peeled and sectioned

¼ cup grape seed oil

2 tablespoons fresh orange juice

½ teaspoon honey (agave or rice syrup for vegans)

½ teaspoon orange zest

Salt and pepper to taste

Preparation:

1. Peel orange with a small knife, removing as much pulp as possible without damaging the fruit.

2. Holding orange over a bowl to catch the juice, run a knife between the membranes. Segment orange, lifting the juicy part of the fruit out of the membrane with the knife. Squeeze the rest of the juice from what is left in the membrane into a small bowl. Set aside.

3. In a small bowl, mix grape seed oil, orange juice, honey, and lemon zest. Season with salt and pepper. In a medium bowl, mix the fennel, sectioned orange pieces, and dressing. Cover, refrigerate, and allow to marinate for 1 hour. Can be prepared a day in advance.

Nutritional information per serving:

197 calories	61 mg sodium
14 g fat	19 g carbohydrates
1 g saturated fat	5 g fiber
0 mg cholesterol	2 g protein

Cool Kale Salad with Cilantro Dressing

ng   gf   v

Kale is one of my favorite greens! The greener the better. Eat it every day, and lots of it!

Ingredients:

4 cups kale, shredded

2 oranges, peeled and sectioned

¾ cup jicama, peeled and diced

½ cup cilantro

3 tablespoons fresh orange juice

1 lime, juiced

¼ cup olive oil

½ cup pumpkin seeds

Salt and pepper to taste

Preparation:

1. In a blender bowl, place cilantro, orange juice, and lime juice. Pulse until finely chopped.

2. With the blender running, slowly drizzle olive oil into the blender bowl in a steady stream until blended well. Season with salt and pepper.

3. In a large bowl, mix shredded kale, sectioned orange, and jicama.

4. Pour the dressing over the kale mixture and toss to coat. Mix in seeds.

5. Refrigerate for 30 minutes before serving.

Nutritional information per serving:

251 calories
16 g fat
2 g saturated fat
0 mg cholesterol

77 mg sodium
27 g carbohydrates
6 g fiber
5 g protein

LIVE AND SATISFYING: SALADS

Mung Bean Salad

v   gf   ng

Ingredients:

¾ cup dry mung beans (Always soak overnight and cook thoroughly. Only use canned beans in a pinch.)

2 tablespoons olive oil

2 tablespoons fresh lemon juice

1 garlic clove, minced

1 tablespoon fresh parsley, chopped

2 tablespoons fresh mint, chopped

2 green onions, chopped

1 red bell pepper, diced

Salt and pepper to taste

Preparation:

1. In a large bowl, cover beans with cold water and soak overnight. Drain and rinse well before cooking.

2. Bring a large pot of water to a boil. Add mung beans, lower heat, cover, and simmer for 15-20 minutes or until beans are tender but not mushy. Drain beans and rinse under cold water.

3. In a large bowl, whisk oil and lemon juice. Add garlic, parsley, and mint.

4. Mix in cooked beans, onions, and red bell pepper. Season with salt and pepper.

Nutritional information per serving:

112 calories	3 mg sodium
7 g fat	10 g carbohydrates
1 g saturated fat	4 g fiber
0 mg cholesterol	3 g protein

Spinach and Strawberry Salad with Pecans

ng gf v

Makes 4 Servings

Ingredients:

3 cups baby spinach

1 cup strawberries, sliced

½ cup pecans

2 tablespoons balsamic vinegar

1 teaspoon honey (agave or rice syrup for vegans)

¼ cup olive oil

Salt to taste

Preparation:

1. In a small bowl, mix balsamic vinegar and honey.

2. Slowly whisk in olive oil. Season with salt. Refrigerate until ready to serve.

3. Spread spinach on plate, top with strawberries and pecans. Drizzle with balsamic vinaigrette and serve.

Nutritional information per serving:

248 calories	21 mg sodium
24 g fat	8 g carbohydrates
3 g saturated fat	3 g fiber
0 mg cholesterol	2 g protein

Brain-Fit Fajita Salad

Makes 4 Servings

gf ng

Ingredients:

2 free-range, hormone-free, boneless, skinless chicken breasts (4-6 ounces), cut into thin strips

1 tablespoon olive oil

1 tablespoon coconut oil

1 lime, juiced

2 garlic cloves, minced

1 teaspoon ground cumin

1 tablespoon fresh oregano, chopped

1 onion, cut into wedges

1 red bell pepper, cut into thin strips

1 can diced green chiles (4 ounces)

3 tomatoes, cut into wedges

1 avocado, sliced

2 tablespoons cilantro, chopped

romaine lettuce leaves, separated

Salt and pepper to taste

Preparation:

1. Rinse chicken and cut off excess fat.

2. In a large bowl, combine olive oil, lime juice, garlic, cumin, oregano, salt, and pepper.

3. Add chicken to the bowl and marinate for 1-24 hours.

4. In a skillet, heat coconut oil over medium-high heat. Add onion and sauté for 2 minutes.

5. Drain chicken, add to the skillet, and cook for 3-4 minutes.

6. Add red pepper and chilies. Cook for an additional 3 minutes or until chicken is cooked through.

7. Serve over lettuce leaves and top with tomatoes, avocado, and cilantro.

Nutritional information per serving:

313 calories	161 mg sodium
16 g fat	15 g carbohydrates
5 g saturated fat	6 g fiber
68 mg cholesterol	30 g protein

Rainbow Quinoa Salad

gf v

Ingredients:

1 cup red quinoa

⅓ cup dried cranberries

4 green onions, chopped

1 cup baby spinach

1 yellow pepper, thinly sliced

1 cup garbanzo beans, rinsed and drained. Always soak overnight and cook thoroughly. (Only use canned beans in a pinch.)

½ cup fresh basil, chopped

¼ cup olive oil

2 tablespoons fresh lemon juice

Zest from 1 lemon

Salt and pepper to taste

Preparation:

1. Rinse quinoa well. Combine quinoa with 2 cups water in a medium pot and bring it to a boil over high heat. Reduce heat, cover, and simmer for 20-30 minutes or until water is absorbed and quinoa is fluffy. Let it cool.

2. In a small bowl, mix olive oil, lemon juice, lemon zest, salt, and pepper.

3. In a large bowl, mix quinoa, cranberries, green onions, yellow pepper, baby spinach, and garbanzo beans.

4. Stir in basil and toss with prepared dressing. Serve chilled or at room temperature.

Nutritional information per serving:

275 calories	128 mg sodium
11 g fat	39 g carbohydrates
1 g saturated fat	6 g fiber
0 mg cholesterol	7 g protein

LIVE AND SATISFYING: SALADS

Stay Sharp Chard Salad

Makes 4 Servings

v gf ng

Ingredients:

3 cups chard, shredded

1 cup green cabbage, shredded

4 tablespoons dried blueberries

1 tablespoon hemp seed oil

½ avocado, diced

½ cup cilantro, chopped

2 tablespoons fresh lime juice

¼ cup soy creamer

2 tablespoons hemp seeds

1 tablespoon fresh basil, chopped

Salt and pepper to taste

Preparation:

1. In a large bowl, mix chard, green cabbage, and blueberries.

2. In a blender bowl or small food processor, place hemp seed oil, avocado, cilantro, lime juice, soy creamer, salt, and pepper. Blend until smooth.

3. Toss the dressing with chard mixture.

4. Sprinkle with hemp seeds and basil, and mix well.

5. Marinate in refrigerator for 1 hour.

Nutritional information per serving:

191 calories	256 mg sodium
11 g fat	20 g carbohydrates
1 g saturated fat	7 g fiber
1 mg cholesterol	6 g protein

SCRUMPTIOUS SIDES
Chapter 8

SCRUMPTIOUS SIDES

Chapter 8

Sides can be added to any meal or prepared as tasty treats between meals. Be conscious of the carb-protein ratio if you are preparing them as snacks. If you are choosing a starchy carb as a snack, round it out with a few nuts, seeds or a low-carb protein bar.

SCRUMPTIOUS SIDES

Herbed Garden Vegetables

Makes 4 Servings

Ingredients:

1 red bell pepper, chopped

2 cups cauliflower, cut into florets

1 zucchini, sliced

1 cup broccoli, cut into florets

1 cup crimini mushrooms, sliced

1 yellow onion, cut in half moons

¼ cup olive oil

2 garlic cloves, minced

1 tablespoon fresh lemon juice

1 teaspoon fresh thyme, chopped

1 tablespoon fresh basil, chopped

Salt and pepper to taste

Preparation:

1. Bring water to a full boil in the bottom of a covered steamer. Add vegetables to the steamer, making sure water does not cover vegetables.

2. Cover and steam vegetable for 3-5 minutes. Do not overcook. Vegetables should remain crisp.

3. While vegetables are steaming, mix garlic, lemon juice, thyme, and basil in a large bowl.

4. Whisk in olive oil. Season with salt and pepper as desired.

5. When vegetables are ready, transfer to the bowl with the dressing and toss to coat. Serve warm.

Nutritional information per serving:

155 calories	22 mg sodium
14 g fat	7 g carbohydrates
2 g saturated fat	3 g fiber
0 mg cholesterol	3 g protein

SCRUMPTIOUS SIDES

Grilled Sweet Potatoes

v   gf   ng

Ingredients:

3 sweet potatoes, peeled

1 tablespoon grape seed oil

1 teaspoon curry or cinnamon (Each spice results in a distinctly different flavor. Kids love it with cinnamon!)

1 teaspoon fresh oregano, chopped

Salt to taste

Preparation:

1. In a large pot, bring a water to boil. Add potatoes and cook for 5-10 minutes.

2. Drain potatoes, transfer to a dish, and cool.

3. Preheat grill to medium-high heat.

4. Cut potatoes lengthwise into wedges, drizzle with grape seed oil, and season with oregano, curry or cinnamon, and salt.

5. Grill until light golden brown on all sides.

Nutritional information per serving:

72 calories	21 mg sodium
2 g fat	12 g carbohydrates
0 g saturated fat	2 g fiber
0 mg cholesterol	1 g protein

Go Green with Sautéed Collard Greens

Makes 3 Servings

v   gf   ng

Ingredients:

8 cups collard greens, rinsed, stems removed, and cut into ribbons

2 tablespoons grape seed oil (preferably) or olive oil

½ cup shallots, diced

3 garlic cloves, minced

½ cup vegetable broth

1 tablespoon balsamic vinegar

Salt and pepper to taste

Preparation:

1. In a large, deep skillet, heat oil over medium heat. Add shallots and garlic, and sauté for 1-2 minutes.

2. Add greens and toss well.

3. Add vegetable broth and balsamic vinegar, and cover. Sauté greens until completely wilted and tender, stirring occasionally, about 8-10 minutes. Season with salt and pepper as desired. Serve hot.

Nutritional information per serving:

103 calories	35 mg sodium
7 g fat	9 g carbohydrates
1 g saturated fat	3 g fiber
0 mg cholesterol	2 g protein

Breaded Eggplant and Squash

Makes 6 Servings

Ingredients:

1 small eggplant, cut into ¼-inch slices

3 summer squash, cut into ¼-inch slices

1 egg, beaten

¼ cup water

1½ cup whole-wheat panko breadcrumbs

¼ cup coconut oil

1 teaspoon garlic salt (or to taste)

Pepper to taste (about 1 teaspoon)

Preparation:

1. In a medium bowl, mix egg and water.

2. Place breadcrumbs on a flat plate.

3. Season vegetables with garlic salt and pepper, then dip in egg mixture (just enough to coat vegetables).

4. Coat both sides in panko breadcrumbs.

5. In a skillet, heat coconut oil over medium heat. Cook vegetables for 2-3 minutes on each side or until golden brown. Serve with salsa.

Nutritional information per serving:

200 calories	198 mg sodium
10 g fat	23 g carbohydrates
8 g saturated fat	5 g fiber
35 mg cholesterol	6 g protein

SCRUMPTIOUS SIDES

175

Roasted Brussels Sprouts

ng **gf** **v**

I love the flavor of this recipe. Brussels sprouts and other cruciferous vegetables are among the healthiest for you for many reasons, but getting people to eat them has always been a challenge. If you've always avoided Brussels sprouts, give this recipe a try and it may turn you into a fan, too.

Ingredients:

1½ pounds Brussels sprouts, halved

2 tablespoons coconut oil

2 leeks, cut in half moons (white parts only)

1 tablespoon fresh dill, chopped

Salt and pepper to taste

Preparation:

1. In a skillet, heat oil over medium heat.

2. Add leeks and sauté for 1 minute.

3. Add Brussels sprouts and cook for 5 minutes, or until nicely roasted outside and tender inside, stirring occasionally.

4. Season with salt and pepper as desired. Sprinkle with fresh dill and serve.

Nutritional information per serving:

106 calories	34 mg sodium
5 g fat	7 g carbohydrates
4 g saturated fat	5 g fiber
0 mg cholesterol	4 g protein

SCRUMPTIOUS SIDES

Surprising Split Pea Hummus

Makes 6 Servings

v gf ng

Why is this recipe so surprising? Because when I serve this tasty hummus to guests, they are always surprised when I tell them it is made with peas. Peas are high in soluble fiber, which has been shown to lower cholesterol and blood glucose levels.

Ingredients:

1 cup dry split peas

2½ cups water

1 bay leaf

2 tablespoons olive oil

1 garlic clove, minced

1 tablespoon fresh lemon juice

1 tablespoon tahini

Salt to taste

Preparation:

1. In a medium pan, place split peas, water, and bay leaf. Bring to a boil. Cover, reduce heat, and simmer for 40 minutes or until peas are tender and liquid is absorbed, stirring occasionally.

2. Take bay leaf out and cool.

3. Add cooked peas, olive oil, garlic, lemon juice, and tahini into a food processor. Process until smooth. Season with salt as desired.

4. Serve with freshly cut vegetables.

Nutritional information per serving:

95 calories	4 mg sodium
6 g fat	8 g carbohydrates
1 g saturated fat	3 g fiber
0 mg cholesterol	3 g protein

Grilled Tofu

Makes 4 Servings   v   gf   ng

Grilled tofu is a good source of vegetarian protein. Use it as a substitute in meat dishes or add it to pasta and salads. This is especially important for vegetarians and vegans who may find it challenging to get the proper amount of complete protein.

Ingredients:

14 ounces extra firm tofu, drained

2 tablespoons rice vinegar

2 garlic cloves, minced

2 tablespoons tamari sauce

1 tablespoon ginger, minced

1 tablespoon honey (agave or rice syrup for vegans)

1 tablespoon sesame oil

Preparation:

1. In a medium bowl, mix rice vinegar, garlic, tamari sauce, ginger, and honey.

2. Cut tofu crosswise into ½-inch thick slices. Place in shallow dish.

3. Pour marinade over tofu and turn to coat. Refrigerate for 1 hour.

4. Preheat grill to medium-high heat and lightly oil the grill rack.

5. Place tofu on a grill rack and cook for 4 minutes on each side. Serve over a bed of mixed greens or baby spinach.

Nutritional information per serving:

108 calories	566 mg sodium
5 g fat	7 g carbohydrates
1 g saturated fat	0 g fiber
0 mg cholesterol	8 g protein

Simply Delicious Guacamole

ng gf v

Ingredients:

2 avocados, peeled, pitted, and diced

1 garlic clove, minced

2 tablespoons fresh lime juice

1 tablespoon cilantro, chopped

Salt to taste

Optional: 1 tomato, diced

Preparation:

1. Mix all ingredients gently.

2. Mash avocados to desired consistency.

3. Serve with freshly cut vegetables.

Nutritional information per serving:

148 calories	7 mg sodium
13 g fat	8 g carbohydrates
2 g saturated fat	6 g fiber
0 mg cholesterol	2 g protein

SCRUMPTIOUS SIDES

Cauliflower with Basil Sauce

Simple and delicious!

Ingredients:

1 large head of cauliflower, cut into 1-inch florets

2 tablespoons coconut oil or grape seed oil

3 ounces fresh basil (about 6 tablespoons)

¼ cup olive oil

1 tablespoon fresh lemon juice

Salt and pepper to taste

Preparation:

1. Bring a large pot of water to a boil.

2. Blanch basil for 30 seconds. Squeeze out water and place in a blender or small food processor.

3. Add olive oil and lemon juice, and purée. Season with salt and pepper as desired.

4. Transfer to a small bowl placed over ice to stop the cooking process.

5. In a large skillet, heat coconut oil or grape seed oil over medium heat. Sauté cauliflower on both sides until golden brown. Drizzle basil sauce on cauliflower and serve.

Nutritional information per serving:

207 calories	64 mg sodium
18 g fat	12 g carbohydrates
7 g saturated fat	6 g fiber
0 mg cholesterol	5 g protein

SCRUMPTIOUS SIDES

Yellow Beans with Tomatoes

Makes 4 Servings   v   gf   ng

Here is a vegetable dish that is so delicious, even your children will love it!

Ingredients:

1 pound fresh yellow beans

1 tablespoon coconut oil

1 small yellow onion, diced

3 garlic cloves, minced

2 Roma tomatoes, diced

2 tablespoons fresh basil, chopped

2 tablespoons walnuts, chopped

Salt and pepper to taste

Preparation:

1. Bring water to a boil in a large pot. Drop in beans and cook for 2 minutes.

2. Transfer beans into a large bowl with ice water to stop the cooking process. Drain beans and set aside.

3. In a large skillet, heat oil over medium heat. Stir in onion and garlic, and cook for 3 minutes.

4. Add tomatoes and cook 1 more minute.

5. Stir in beans and cook until warmed through.

6. Mix in basil and walnuts, and season with salt and pepper as desired.

Nutritional information per serving:

231 calories	276 mg sodium
7 g fat	32 g carbohydrates
4 g saturated fat	13 g fiber
0 mg cholesterol	12 g protein

Succulent Roasted Sweet Potatoes

IIIIIIIIIIIIIIIIIIIIIIIIIIIIIIIIIIIIIIIIIIIIIIIIIIIIIIIIIIIIIIIIIIIIIIIIIIIIIIIIIIIIIIIIIIIIIIIIIIIIIIII

Makes 6 Servings　　　　　　　　　　　v　　gf　　ng

Ingredients:

3 sweet potatoes, peeled and sliced in rounds

1 tablespoon grape seed oil or olive oil

½ teaspoon salt

1 teaspoon cinnamon

½ cup raisins or cranberries

Preparation:

1. Preheat oven to 375 degrees F.

2. Place potatoes in a 9 x 13-inch baking dish. Drizzle with oil. Sprinkle with salt, cinnamon, and raisins. Toss to coat.

3. Arrange potatoes in rows in baking dish and roast for 35-40 minutes or until tender and golden brown.

Nutritional information per serving:

143 calories	228 mg sodium
2 g fat	30 g carbohydrates
0 g saturated fat	4 g fiber
0 mg cholesterol	2 g protein

SCRUMPTIOUS SIDES

DECEIVINGLY DECADENT: DESSERTS

Chapter 9

We all love a decadent treat now and then, and there is no reason why you can't enjoy an occasional treat. The key is breaking your addiction to sugar! But how can you do that when your taste buds and metabolism have been hijacked by the sugar-filled, fat-laden treats the food industry has programmed you to eat? To kick the habit, you need to re-learn to love the natural sweet taste of foods that have not been processed with massive amounts of sugar, fat, and salt. The wholesome and natural desserts in this section will help you re-activate your taste buds. With your taste buds turned on, you will be amazed at how sweet and delicious natural flavors can be!

Remember, these desserts are designed to be a treat, not a meal! That means *very small* portions. Indulging only occasionally will help you break your addiction to sweets. The more carbs you eat, the more you want. Some of the desserts are not low in fat, but they are low in refined sugar. Remember, it's not fat (at least not the right fat) that makes you fat, it's sugar that makes you fat... and too many calories!

Fruit Granita

ng gf v

Live, luscious, and so easy to make! This one is great anytime!

Ingredients:

3 cups raspberries, strawberries, or blueberries (or a combination)

½ cup water

1 tablespoon fresh lemon juice

1-2 mint leaves

10 drops apricot-flavored liquid stevia

Preparation:

1. Put all ingredients in a blender and process until smooth. Pour mixture into a shallow baking dish.

2. Cover and freeze until mixture is crystallized, stirring every 20 or 30 minutes and scraping sides with a fork.

3. Remove from freezer and scrape with a fork to "shave" into flakes. Serve in chilled glasses. Garnish with mint.

Nutritional information per serving:

46 calories	0 mg sodium
1 g fat	11 g carbohydrates
0 g saturated fat	6 g fiber
0 mg cholesterol	1 g protein

DECEIVINGLY DECADENT: DESSERTS

Amazing Avocado Gelato

ng gf v

Avocado gelato? Yes, it may sound a bit weird, but I haven't met a kid yet who doesn't LOVE it. Avocado gelato is a lower-sugar, lighter-calorie adaptation of a recipe from my friend Jenny Ross, who owns the raw-food restaurant 118 Degrees. Raw, live, and luscious!

Ingredients:

3 avocados

¼ cup coconut butter

¼ cup honey (agave or rice syrup for vegans)

3 tablespoons sugar-free chocolate protein powder (vegan)

2 tablespoons raw cacao powder

½ cup almond milk, unsweetened

3 tablespoons coconut flakes, unsweetened

1 dropper full chocolate-flavored liquid stevia

Preparation:

1. In a blender, mix all the ingredients except coconut flakes. Blend until creamy and smooth. Mixture should be very thick!

2. Either smooth entire contents into a cake pan or drop round in tablespoon-sized balls (like cookies, but a little thinner) onto a cookie sheet. Note that it is easier to spread the mixture into a cake pan, but it is a little more challenging to cut it after it has been frozen. Dropping onto a cookie sheet can be a little messy, but then it is easier to grab and eat after freezing. Try it both ways and see how you like it.

3. Sprinkle coconut over the top.

4. Place cake pan or cookie sheet in freezer for at least 2 hours until frozen.

5. Serve as a frozen treat. They taste like Fudgesicles!

Nutritional information per serving:

162 calories	23 mg sodium
11 g fat	14 g carbohydrates
4 g saturated fat	4 g fiber
0 mg cholesterol	6 g protein

DECEIVINGLY DECADENT: DESSERTS

Warm Sweet Potato Pudding

Makes 6 Servings

v gf ng

Yum! I love this dessert because it is so scrumptious. It's also very low in added refined sugar, and it contains absolutely no grains or flour. It is one of the healthiest desserts you can eat. Because it tastes so great and is so good for you, you may be tempted to overindulge. But remember: when it comes to food, there can be too much of a good thing. Think small portions here.

Ingredients:

1 pound sweet potatoes, peeled and cubed

1 Bosc pear, cored and cubed

¾ teaspoon ground cinnamon

⅛ teaspoon ground nutmeg

¼ cup pure maple syrup

¼ cup macadamia nuts

2 tablespoons coconut butter

1 tablespoon coconut flakes, unsweetened

Preparation:

1. Fill the bottom of a large pot with water. Place a steamer basket in the bottom of the pot, making sure that the basket isn't covered by the water. Bring the water to a full boil. Add sweet potatoes and pear to the steamer basket. Cover and steam sweet potatoes and pear until very tender, about 10-15 minutes.

2. Put macadamia nuts in a food processor and pulse until they are a fine consistency.

3. Add steamed sweet potatoes, pear, cinnamon, nutmeg, and maple syrup to the processor and mix until all ingredients are blended well and smooth.

4. Sprinkle with coconut flakes and serve warm.

Nutritional information per serving:

197 calories	32 mg sodium
9 g fat	30 g carbohydrates
5 g saturated fat	4 g fiber
0 mg cholesterol	3 g protein

Grilled Peaches

Makes 4 Servings

v gf ng

Can you say delicious? Fruit becomes sugar when it is cooked, and I find that the peaches in this recipe taste plenty sweet without the optional honey or agave syrup. Try it that way first. You may be surprised to find that you don't need to add anything to satisfy your sweet tooth.

Ingredients:

4 peaches, halved and pitted

1 tablespoon grape seed oil

Optional: 2 tablespoons honey or agave syrup

Preparation:

1. Preheat the grill to medium-high heat.

2. Brush peaches with oil.

3. Lightly oil grill racks. Place peaches cut side down. Grill 2-4 minutes or until you get grill marks and fruit is tender. Turn over and grill the other side. Drizzle 1-2 teaspoons of honey or agave syrup on each peach if desired.

Nutritional information per serving:

72 calories	0 mg sodium
3 g fat	11 g carbohydrates
0 g saturated fat	2 g fiber
0 mg cholesterol	1 g protein

Peach Coconut Cream Delight

Ingredients:

Meat of 1 young Thai coconut

2 large peaches, cut into wedges

1 tablespoon coconut butter

1 teaspoon ginger, minced

2 tablespoons sugar-free vanilla protein powder (we prefer pea protein)

¼ cup macadamia nuts

20 drops vanilla crème- or apricot-flavored liquid stevia

Optional: 1 tablespoon raw honey (agave or rice syrup for vegans)

Preparation:

1. Crack open the top of the coconut using the heavy end of a meat cleaver. Letting the weight of the cleaver strike the outer quarter of the coconut, form a square around the top. Continue circling the top until it cracks and the top can be lifted out with the cleaver.

2. Pour the coconut water into a bowl.

3. Using the edge of a spoon, gently scrape the inside of the coconut to remove the meat. The younger the coconut, the more tender the meat.

4. Put ¼ cup coconut water, coconut meat, peaches, coconut butter, ginger, protein powder, and macadamia nuts in a blender and process until smooth. Refrigerate for 2 hours for pudding consistency or freeze for frozen dessert. Sprinkle with shredded coconut and serve chilled.

Nutritional information per serving:

163 calories	25 mg sodium
12 g fat	12 g carbohydrates
6 g saturated fat	4 g fiber
0 mg cholesterol	4 g protein

DECEIVINGLY DECADENT: DESSERTS

201

ng **gf** **v**

These simple, raw treats are one of my favorites. Loaded with superfoods and antioxidants, they are intended to be a tasty "morsel." A little dollop will do!

Ingredients:

¼ cup goji powder

¼ cup vegan vanilla-flavored protein powder (sweetened with stevia)

½ cup raw macadamia nuts

2 tablespoons cacao butter, melted

¼ cup raw honey (agave or maple syrup for vegans)

5-10 drops chocolate-flavored liquid stevia

¼ cup raw cacao nibs

¼ cup whole goji berries

½ cup shredded coconut

Optional: Zest from 1 orange

Preparation:

1. Place goji powder, protein powder, and macadamia nuts into a food processor. Pulse several times until blended.

2. While ingredients are blending, slowly add melted cacao butter, honey, and stevia in a steady stream. Be sure not to dump all the liquid at once into dry mixture. Blend until mixture is smooth and creamy. Transfer mixture to a medium-sized bowl.

3. By hand, blend in cacao nibs, goji berries, and orange zest. Mix thoroughly.

4. Form into teaspoon-sized balls and roll in coconut.

5. Place on a cookie sheet. Mixture should yield 16 truffles. Refrigerate for 1 hour.

Nutritional information per serving:

64 calories	78 mg sodium
7 g fat	10 g carbohydrates
3 g saturated fat	2 g fiber
0 mg cholesterol	7 g protein

DECEIVINGLY DECADENT: DESSERTS

Rice Power Pudding

Makes 6 Servings

v gf

This wholesome twist on a traditional favorite is so silky smooth and creamy, you won't even notice the beneficial boost you're getting from the fiber and protein. Add nuts and fruit to turn it into a tasty breakfast meal.

Ingredients:

1 cup brown rice

4 cups almond milk, unsweetened

1 vanilla bean, halved and scraped

2 tablespoons vanilla or chocolate protein powder

2 tablespoons raisins

1 apple, peeled and diced

1 teaspoon ground cinnamon

2 tablespoons raw almonds or walnuts, chopped

5-10 drops cinnamon-flavored liquid stevia

Preparation:

1. In a medium saucepan, mix rice, almond milk, vanilla, raisins, and apple. Bring to a boil. Reduce heat, cover, and simmer for 50-60 minutes or until thickened, stirring occasionally.

2. Add protein powder after pudding has cooled some. Mix well.

3. Add stevia to desired sweetness. Serve warm or chilled.

4. Sprinkle with cinnamon and nuts before serving.

Nutritional information per serving:

100 calories	102 mg sodium
2 g fat	19 g carbohydrates
0 g saturated fat	2 g fiber
0 mg cholesterol	2 g protein

ng gf v

Here's one for all of you "chocoholics." This is one great-tasting dessert that contains very little sugar and no grains while providing a significant amount of protein.

Ingredients:

1½ cups silken tofu, drained

2 tablespoons cacao powder

2 tablespoons coconut butter

1 tablespoon honey (agave or rice syrup for vegans)

½ cup walnuts

2 tablespoons coconut flakes

20 drops chocolate-flavored liquid stevia

Preparation:

1. In a blender bowl, place tofu, cacao powder, stevia, coconut butter, honey, and walnuts. Blend until smooth.

2. Transfer to a bowl and chill in the refrigerator for 1 hour.

3. Scoop mousse into martini glasses and garnish with coconut flakes.

Nutritional information per serving:

171 calories	44 mg sodium
16 g fat	14 g carbohydrates
6 g saturated fat	4 g fiber
0 mg cholesterol	7 g protein

DECEIVINGLY DECADENT: DESSERTS

Carrot Zucchini Muffins

v gf

Looking for a way to sneak some veggies into your kids' snacks? Say hello to the healthiest muffins I've ever made. They get rave reviews from kids... and their parents! They're such a hit, we serve them instead of birthday cake at kids' parties, and everybody loves them.

Ingredients:

1 cup carrots, grated

1 cup zucchini, grated

¼ cup grape seed oil

¼ cup honey (agave or rice syrup for vegans)

¾ cup almond milk, unsweetened

1 cup all-purpose gluten-free flour

1 cup oat flour

2 teaspoons cinnamon

¼ teaspoon nutmeg

1 teaspoon baking soda

1 teaspoon baking powder

¼ cup chia seeds

½ cup prunes, chopped

Preparation:

1. Preheat oven to 350 degrees F.

2. In a large bowl, mix flour, oat flour, cinnamon, nutmeg, baking soda, baking powder, chia seeds, and prunes.

3. In a small bowl, mix grape seed oil, honey, and almond milk. Add to flour mixture.

4. Stir in carrots and zucchini.

5. Lightly oil 12-cup muffin pan.

6. Spoon batter evenly between muffin pan cups.

7. Bake for 25-35 minutes or until golden brown. A toothpick inserted into the center of a muffin should come out clean.

Nutritional information per serving:

165 calories	123 mg sodium
7 g fat	27 g carbohydrates
1 g saturated fat	4 g fiber
0 mg cholesterol	3 g protein

Gluten-free cobbler? When I first tried this amazing recipe, I couldn't believe it was gluten-free. Plus, it's filled with "brainberries"—that's what Daniel calls antioxidant-rich blueberries because they are so good for brain health.

Ingredients:

6 cups organic blueberries

1 teaspoon arrowroot

2 tablespoons honey (agave or rice syrup for vegans)

1 cup all-purpose gluten-free flour

½ cup brown rice flour

1 teaspoon baking powder

1 cup almond milk, unsweetened

Preparation:

1. Preheat oven to 375 degrees F.

2. In a medium bowl, combine all-purpose flour, brown rice flour, baking soda, and milk. Set aside.

3. Place blueberries into a 9 x 9-inch baking dish. Toss arrowroot with berries.

4. Drizzle with honey.

5. Pour the batter over berries.

6. Bake cobbler for 45 minutes or until the top is golden brown. Serve warm.

DECEIVINGLY DECADENT: DESSERTS

Nutritional information per serving:

173 calories	88 mg sodium
1 g fat	40 g carbohydrates
0 g saturated fat	5 g fiber
0 mg cholesterol	3 g protein

Poached Pears with Carob Sauce

Makes 4 Servings

v   gf   ng

Chocolate lovers rejoice! Carob offers all that rich chocolate taste with just half the sugar and half the fat of regular chocolate.

Ingredients:

4 firm Bosc pears, peeled, core removed, stem intact

4 cups water

2 tablespoons honey (agave or rice syrup for vegans)

3 whole cloves

1 vanilla bean, split and scraped

¼ cup soy creamer

2 tablespoons carob chips

Preparation:

1. In a medium saucepan, combine water, honey, clove, and vanilla bean. Bring to a boil. Reduce heat and simmer for 5 minutes.

2. Place pears in hot liquid, cover, and simmer for 15-20 minutes or until very tender. Remove pears from liquid and let cool.

3. In a small saucepan, mix soy creamer and carob chips. Warm over medium-low heat, whisking constantly until the carob is melted. Be careful not to burn carob.

4. Drizzle a small amount of sauce over pears and serve. Discard remaining sauce.

Nutritional information per serving:

180 calories	35 mg sodium
3 g fat	39 g carbohydrates
1 g saturated fat	5 g fiber
0 mg cholesterol	2 g protein

DECEIVINGLY DECADENT: DESSERTS

Fresh Berries with Macadamia Nut Sauce

ng **gf** **v**

This raw macadamia nut sauce is adapted from a recipe from Jenny Ross, the owner of the wildly popular raw-food restaurant 118 Degrees. We became friends after I fell in love with the food there. Kamila and I have been taking "non-cooking" lessons from her ever since. Raw, living food is a true art form.

Ingredients:

1 cup fresh blueberries

1 cup fresh strawberries, sliced

1 cup fresh raspberries

½ cup macadamia nuts

2 tablespoons coconut flakes

½ cup light coconut milk

10 drops vanilla crème-flavored liquid stevia

Optional: 1 tablespoon honey (agave or rice syrup for vegans)

Preparation:

1. In a large bowl, gently toss berries.

2. In a blender bowl, add macadamia nuts, coconut flakes, coconut milk, stevia, and honey (if desired). Blend until smooth and creamy. If sauce is too thick, add 2-4 tablespoons unsweetened milk until sauce reaches desired consistency.

3. Transfer berries to serving bowls and drizzle with nut sauce.

Nutritional information per serving:

273 calories	10 mg sodium
23 g fat	21 g carbohydrates
4 g saturated fat	6 g fiber
0 mg cholesterol	3 g protein

Oatmeal Cookies with Goji Berries

gf v

Ingredients:

1 cup all-purpose gluten-free flour

1 cup gluten-free rolled oats

1 teaspoon baking powder

1 teaspoon baking soda

½ teaspoon cinnamon

½ cup goji berries, chopped

1 egg

2 tablespoons grape seed oil

¼ cup honey (agave or rice syrup for vegans)

1 teaspoon vanilla extract

⅓ puréed apple

Preparation:

1. In a large bowl, mix flour, oats, baking powder, baking soda, and cinnamon. Stir in goji berries.

2. In a small bowl, whisk egg, grape seed oil, honey, vanilla, and puréed apple. Combine the wet ingredients with the dry ingredients and mix until blended well. Cover and refrigerate for 30-60 minutes.

3. Preheat the oven to 375 degrees F.

4. Line a baking sheet with parchment paper. Drop teaspoon-sized balls of batter onto the lined cookie sheet. Bake for 10-12 minutes or until golden brown.

Nutritional information per serving:

182 calories	60 mg sodium
4 g fat	33 g carbohydrates
1 g saturated fat	4 g fiber
21 mg cholesterol	5 g protein

Coco Goji Pudding

Super tasty and loaded with nutrition. Goji berries are a "superfood," filled with phytonutrients and antioxidants. The addition of protein powder makes this a great option for breakfast too.

Ingredients:

Meat of 2 Thai coconuts (save the juice)

¼ cup coconut water

¼ cup almond milk, unsweetened

1 tablespoon raw honey (agave or rice syrup for vegans)

1 scoop sugar-free vanilla protein powder (vegan)

¼ teaspoon sea salt

Optional: 5 drops vanilla crème-flavored liquid stevia

Optional: 2 tablespoons carob chips

Preparation:

1. Crack open the tops of the coconuts using the heavy end of a meat cleaver. Letting the weight of the cleaver strike the outer quarter of the coconut, form a square around the top. Continue circling the top until it cracks and the top can be lifted out with the cleaver.

2. Pour out the coconut water and reserve.

3. Using the edge of a spoon, gently scrape the inside of the coconut to remove the meat. The younger the coconut, the more tender the meat.

4. Place all ingredients except carob chips into a blender bowl and blend until smooth and creamy.

5. Scoop pudding mixture into serving bowls, top with carob chips, and chill for 30 minutes before serving.

Nutritional information per serving:

119 calories	197 mg sodium
7 g fat	10 g carbohydrates
6 g saturated fat	3 g fiber
0 mg cholesterol	6 g protein

DECEIVINGLY DECADENT: DESSERTS

AMEN FAMILY HOLIDAY MEAL

Chapter 10

AMEN FAMILY HOLIDAY MEAL

Chapter 10

Have you ever noticed that "flu season" always seems to strike during the holidays? One of the most obvious explanations is the extreme change in our diet. Most people use the holidays as an excuse to gorge on excessive amounts of sugar, fat, and salt. When eaten in excess, these foods trigger an inflammatory response, leading to a breakdown in the ability of your body to fight disease.

Typically what I see served at most holiday dinners are lots of fatty, sugary foods, and one token vegetable dish (and even that is usually covered with salt and sugar). I recently read that Thanksgiving is the day of the year when the most heart attacks happen. That's hardly something to be thankful for. Reportedly, people eat up to 4,000 calories each on this day of gratitude. This is a tremendous burden for any body.

The secret to feeling fabulous during the holidays is to follow an anti-inflammatory diet. How does this look on your holiday table? In the Amen household it means we have a beautiful turkey in the middle of the table, surrounded by a variety of delicious vegetable dishes (candied yams don't count as a vegetable) and salads. We typically follow the same 70/30 rule we follow all year long: 70 percent water-rich live foods and 30 percent concentrated foods.

Here are several mouth-watering recipes that we eat at the Amen household. Maybe they'll become favorites in your family too.

Smarter Stuffing

v

Ingredients:

1-2 tablespoons Earth Balance® (a butter replacement)

2 cups stuffing bread (try making your own from whole-grain or gluten-free bread)

½ cup onion, finely chopped

½ cup carrots, diced

½ cup celery, finely chopped

3 cloves garlic, minced

¼ cup apple, chopped

¼ cup walnuts, chopped

¼ cup raisins or cranberries

2 cups low-sodium vegetable broth or chicken broth

Salt and pepper to taste

Optional: 1-2 teaspoons fresh thyme

Optional: 1-2 teaspoons fresh rosemary

Optional: 1-2 teaspoons fresh marjoram

Optional: 1 teaspoon allspice

Preparation:

1. Preheat oven to 350 degrees F.

2. Over medium heat, melt Earth Balance®. Add carrots and onions, and sauté for 1 minute. Add celery and garlic, and sauté for 2 more minutes or until slightly soft. Add apple and sauté for 1 more minute. Remove from heat and set aside to cool.

3. In a large bowl, mix bread stuffing, veggies, apple, raisins (or cranberries), and walnuts. Toss together with a little salt and pepper and your favorite herbs.

4. Add broth until moist. Don't add so much broth that the mixture is soaking.

5. Grease a baking dish with Earth Balance® and place stuffing mixture in dish. Cover and bake about 20 minutes. Uncover and cook an additional 10 minutes. Stuffing should have a nice crisp texture on top.

Nutritional information per serving:

227 calories	495 mg sodium
12 g fat	28 g carbohydrates
2 g saturated fat	4 g fiber
0 mg cholesterol	4 g protein

Tana's Marinated Turkey

Makes 12 Servings

gf   ng

This recipe requires marinating the turkey overnight prior to cooking. This makes enough marinade for a large turkey. You may not need to use it all for smaller birds. I don't add stuffing to the turkey when cooking because it increases the cooking time too much. You certainly can, but plan to put your turkey in the oven very early.

Ingredients:

1 12-pound free-range, hormone-free, antibiotic-free turkey

½ cup extra virgin olive oil

¼ cup fresh lemon juice

2 tablespoons minced garlic

2 tablespoons fresh rosemary, finely chopped

2 tablespoons fresh thyme, finely chopped

1 tablespoons sea salt, or to taste (reduce amount for low-sodium diet)

1 tablespoon pepper, or to taste

Preparation for the Day Before Cooking:

1. Start with a fully thawed turkey.

2. Remove innards from cavity (set aside for stuffing if desired) and rinse turkey well. Pat dry with paper towels.

3. "Deglove" the skin from the turkey, being careful not to remove the skin from the turkey. You just want to separate the skin from the meat. Try not to puncture the skin. The skin will remain attached at the legs' attachment points.

4. Mix marinade well with a whisk prior to marinating turkey.

5. Evenly apply marinade around turkey meat, under the skin with clean hands (always being careful to handle ALL meat with clean hands and not touch anything else prior to washing). Be sure to apply a thick coat of marinade.

6. Apply a final, thin coat of marinade to the outside of turkey, covering the skin.

7. Use the remaining marinade to apply a thin coat to the inside cavity. If you don't have enough left, you may choose to use sea salt with a little olive oil.

8. Cover turkey and refrigerate overnight.

Preparation for Cooking Day:

1. Preheat oven to 400 degrees F.

2. Place turkey breast-side down (for the most moist breast meat) in a roasting pan or directly on the lower rack above a roasting pan.

3. Cooking time varies, but a general rule is about 15 minutes per pound.

4. After 30 minutes, reduce cooking temperature to 350 degrees F for the next 2 hours, then reduce it again to 250 degrees F for the remaining time.

5. Use a baster to retrieve juices from the bottom of the pan and baste turkey every 30 minutes or so. If there are not enough drippings you may use a little raw, organic melted butter mixed with chicken broth.

6. Use a meat thermometer to ensure meat is fully cooked. The white meat should have a temperature of about 165 degrees F.

7. For the last 20 minutes of cooking time, turn turkey over and turn the temperature up to 300 degrees F. This will brown the skin of the breast.

Roast Chicken Option:

To adapt this turkey recipe for roast chicken, cut ingredients in half and marinate according to the same instructions. Preheat oven to 425 degrees F and roast for 1½ hours. Keep chicken breast-side down for the first hour and turn over for the final 30 minutes.

Nutritional information:

Nutritional information varies with each part of the turkey. Skinless is recommended for lower calories and lower fat content.

AMEN FAMILY HOLIDAY MEAL

Smooth Sweet Potato Soup

Makes 8 Servings

v   gf   ng

Ingredients:

½ cup onion, diced

⅓ cup celery, diced

3 tablespoons leeks, diced

2 garlic cloves, minced

6-7 cups vegetable stock

1½ pounds sweet potatoes, peeled and diced

1 cinnamon stick

¼ teaspoon nutmeg

1 teaspoon Real Salt

1 teaspoon white pepper

½ cup almond milk

2 tablespoons fresh sage, finely chopped

⅛ cup cranberries

Cinnamon, sprinkled for garnish

Optional: ¼ cup sunflower seeds

Preparation:

1. Heat ¼ cup of vegetable broth in large soup pot over medium heat. Sauté onions, celery, and leeks for 2 minutes. Then add garlic and sauté for another minute.

2. Add 4 cups of remaining vegetable broth, sweet potatoes, cinnamon stick, and nutmeg. Bring to a boil then reduce heat to medium-low and simmer until potatoes are tender, about 10 minutes.

3. Remove cinnamon stick.

4. Use immersion blender or pour contents into a blender in batches. Blend until smooth.

5. Pour soup back into pot (if using a blender). Add almond milk. Then slowly add remaining broth according to preferred consistency.

6. Add salt and pepper.

7. Dish soup into bowls. Sprinkle sunflower seeds, sage, and cranberries in each bowl and serve.

Nutritional information per serving:

81 calories	4 mg sodium
0 g fat	17 g carbohydrates
0 g saturated fat	2 g fiber
0 mg cholesterol	2 g protein

CLEVER KALE SLAW

ng **gf** **v**

Ingredients:

3 cups shredded kale or Swiss chard

½ cup shredded green cabbage

½ cup shredded purple cabbage

¼ cup shredded carrot

½ cup chopped raw cashews

½ cup Veganaise®

1 tablespoon apple cider vinegar

½ teaspoon allspice

⅛ teaspoon cinnamon

⅛ teaspoon nutmeg

1 teaspoon fresh oregano, finely chopped (or ½ teaspoon dried)

1 teaspoon fresh thyme (or ½ teaspoon dried)

⅓ teaspoon curry powder

¼ teaspoon Real Salt

¼ teaspoon pepper

¼ cup raw sunflower seeds

½ cup dried cranberries

Optional: Use 1 cup prepackaged coleslaw mix instead of cabbage

Optional: ½ packet stevia

Preparation:

1. Combine kale, cabbage, carrot, and nuts.

2. In a small mixing bowl, combine Vegenaise®, vinegar, stevia, herbs, and spices. Whisk until mixture is blended well.

3. Toss with salad mix.

4. Allow salad to refrigerate for 30 minutes prior to serving if possible, so flavors can "marry."

5. Top with sunflower seeds and dried cranberries.

Nutritional information per serving:

201 calories
14 g fat
2 g saturated fat
0 mg cholesterol

187 mg sodium
14 g carbohydrates
3 g fiber
3 g protein

CAULIFLOWER MASHED "POTATOES"

Ingredients:

1 head cauliflower

2 cups vegetable broth or water

¼ cup soy milk or almond milk, unsweetened

1 tablespoon Earth Balance®

½ teaspoon Italian seasoning

2 clove garlic, minced

1 teaspoon fresh rosemary, chopped

2 teaspoons cornstarch mixed with 2 tablespoons water

2 cups spinach

¼ cup sunflower seeds

Salt and pepper to taste.

Optional: 2 tablespoons chives, finely chopped

Preparation:

1. Pour vegetable broth into a medium-sized pot. Put cauliflower florets in pot and bring to a boil over medium-high heat. Cover, reduce heat to low, and simmer for 10 minutes. If you prefer using water, steam cauliflower in a steamer basket, being sure not to allow the water to bathe the cauliflower. If steaming, cook until fork tender, about 8 minutes.

2. While cauliflower is cooking, combine soy or almond milk, Earth Balance®, garlic, Italian seasoning, and rosemary in a small saucepan over medium heat. When it reaches a boil, add cornstarch/water mixture, stirring constantly until it is thickened and smooth. Remove from heat and set aside.

3. Drain as much liquid from cauliflower as possible and place florets in a food processor or blender, blending on high for about 1 minute. Add sauce, and blend until smooth and creamy.

4. Add salt and pepper to taste.

5. Add sunflower seeds and chives if desired, and serve hot over a bed of spinach.

Nutritional information per serving:

435 calories	590 mg sodium
35 g fat	29 g carbohydrates
25 g saturated fat	11 g fiber
0 mg cholesterol	10 g protein

Sassy Cucumber Mint Salad

ng **gf** **v**

Ingredients:

1 bunch mint, stems removed

1 bunch parsley, stems removed

2 cucumbers, minced

1 red bell pepper, finely chopped

6 scallions, minced

4 tomatoes, seeded and finely chopped

½ cup fresh lemon juice

¼ cup olive oil

½ teaspoon Real Salt

½ teaspoon paprika

Preparation:

1. Finely mince mint and parsley by hand or in food processor, if preferred.

2. In large mixing bowl, blend herbs with cucumber, bell pepper, scallions, and tomatoes.

3. Add lemon juice, olive oil, and spices.

4. Toss and serve.

Nutritional information per serving:

130 calories	205 mg sodium
9 g fat	12 g carbohydrates
2 g saturated fat	3 g fiber
0 mg cholesterol	2 g protein

AMEN FAMILY HOLIDAY MEAL

TWO-WEEK SUCCESS MENU
Chapter 12

The following is a two-week sample menu to help you get started on your journey to success. This menu is to help you see just how often you should be eating and how diverse your weekly menu can be. This is not a boring menu! With a little creativity, there are as many options as there are days in a year.

If you are anything like me, you are probably pretty busy and on the run all the time! In all honesty, I do not eat this way every day. My menu is a bit less complex than this for the simple reason that I am a creature of habit. My staple foods do not change much... LOTS OF VEGETABLES! However, the meal that is always diverse in our house is dinner. We make sure to make enough so that I automatically have lunch made for the next day. This saves me a lot of time.

I have been called the "food police" more than once, so I want to be careful to meet you where you are, and not to go overboard. Many of the recipes in this cookbook are versatile so you can adapt them according where you are on your journey. If you aren't quite ready to ditch all bread and refined carbs, you may eat some of the wraps and burgers with buns or tortillas.

As you progress, try eating them "open faced" (half the bread) or with lettuce wraps instead. For best results, you should cut as much bread and refined carbs out of your diet as early in your program as possible. They are literally the drug that controls your hormonal balance. Within a week of not eating them, you will likely not miss them at all.

TWO-WEEK SUCCESS MENU

Tana's Menu Tips

Tip 1: Eat breakfast within one hour of waking.

Tip 2: Meals should be about three hours apart. You should not let yourself get hungry.

Tip 3: Measure all portions according to the recipes in the cookbook section.

Tip 4: Women should eat protein portions approximately 3-4 oz in size, or 15-20 grams.

Tip 5: Men should eat protein portions approximately 4-6 oz in size, 20-25 grams.

Tip 6: If there is not a nutritional chart available, estimate portion sizes by using the palm of your hand. Your protein portion should not exceed the size of the palm of your hand, including depth.

Tip 7: Try to limit breads and refined carbohydrates as much as possible for the first two weeks in order to break your addiction to sugar.

Tip 8: Make your carbs "whole" or "sprouted grains" as much as possible. This includes quinoa, brown rice, barley, farro, steel cut oats, etc.

Tip 9: Eat grains like a condiment. Limit all grain consumption to no more than ½ cup servings at one time. Your body can process this amount more easily.

Tip 10: Eat some protein and healthy fat with grains to slow down absorption of sugar.

Tip 11: Try eating sandwiches "open faced" (with one piece of bread only).

Tip 12: Never use white bread.

Tip 13: Try to use Ezekiel bread when possible. It is sprouted grain and flourless.

Tip 14: If using hamburger buns, use Oroweat Multi-Grain Sandwich Thins® brand. It is thin and only has 100 calories for both sides (less than half the calories). Even better if you eat it open faced.

Tip 15: Drink 16 oz of water before meals.

Tip 16: Salads listed in this chapter call for 1 Tbsp of oil with either balsamic vinegar or lemon juice added.

Tip 17: The nuts and seeds are strategically placed in the menu plan to help increase satiety, boost omega-3 fatty acids, and prevent gluconeogenesis (the conversion of muscle to glucose during weight loss).

Tip 18: If you still feel hungry, increase your raw vegetable intake. They are nearly "free" calories. It takes almost as much energy to digest them as they contain. And you get the benefit of a gazillion micronutrients. It's NOT the same with fruit!

Tip 19: If really, REALLY are going to cheat, do it with protein. Don't do it with carbs. I repeat... DO NOT cheat with carbs even though they may count for equal or less calories. Calories are not equal in this game. Protein will increase satiety and drive insulin down. Carbs will cause insulin to rise.

Tip 20: The vegetarian meals by necessity contain more grains and carbs, but as little as we could get away with. It's a balancing act between not using too much soy or grains. My suggestion to vegetarians would be to eat a whole lot of raw and lightly cooked vegetables, only a little in the way of grains and tofu, and increase things like nuts, seed, hemp, chia seeds, etc. There may not be quite as much variety in your meal plan, but what you eat will be nutritious, delicious, and vitalizing. Make Shiritaki noodles one of your staples! You can dress them up in a thousand combinations.

Tip 21: Most of the recipes give options to use Shiritaki noodles instead of pasta. I strongly suggest this! These are free calories (they are virtually calorie-free), compared to pasta which is loaded with calories and carbs (a.k.a. sugar). These will fill your tummy without bankrupting your calorie allowance.

Tip 22: When possible, use a couple of romaine lettuce leaves for "wraps" instead of tortillas or pitas.

Tip 23: Don't view the reduction in carbs as deprivation. Your calorie intake isn't changing just because we removed the carbs. If you cut out the bread you get to add more protein, nuts or even a little fruit. These things will do far more to nourish you and increase your feeling of satisfaction.

WEEK 1 SUCCESS MENU

	BREAKFAST	SNACK	LUNCH
DAY 1	Berry Alert Brain-Boosting Smoothie	¼ cup raw almonds or sunflower seeds	Amazing Apple Cinnamon Chicken Salad
DAY 2	Feel-Good Eggs Ranchero	½ cup berries	Seared Ahi with Cucumber Salad
DAY 3	Green Apple Goddess BrainBoosting Smoothie	¼ cup raw nuts or seeds	Mixed green salad with grilled chicken breast with 1 tablespoon olive oil balsamic dressing
DAY 4	Guilt-Free Granola	Low-carb protein bar	Get Fit Fennel and Orange Salad with added chicken breast
DAY 5	Very Omega Cherry Brain Boosting Smoothie	¼ cup nuts or seeds	Spinach and Strawberry Salad with Pecans with added shrimp
DAY 6	Coco Chunky Monkey Brain-Boosting Smoothie	Chopped veggies with Surprising Split Pea Hummus	Tasty Turkey Wrap
DAY 7	Seafood Omelet for Super Focus with ¼ cup berries	¼ cup raw nuts or seeds	Stay Sharp Chard Salad with added chicken breast

WEEK 1 SUCCESS MENU

SNACK	DINNER	DESSERT
2 cups mixed veggies with 1 tablespoon hummus	The Best Beef Stroganoff	2 oz. Amazing Avocado Gelato
Large mixed green salad with 1 tablespoon sunflower seeds and 1 tablespoon olive oil and lemon juice	Sizzling Chicken and Veggie Kabobs	¼ cup Fruit Granita
1 crisp pear and 2 tablespoons raw nuts or seeds	"Spaghetti" with Turkey Meatballs and steamed broccoli	Brain on Joy bar available at www.amenclinics.com
½ cup berries of your choice and ¼ cup raw almonds	Simple Shrimp Scampi and Vegetable Soup	½ oz. extra dark chocolate (NOT MILK CHOCOLATE)
2 cups raw vegetables with 2 tablespoons guacamole	Memory-Boosting Eggplant Moussaka with 2 cups steamed vegetables	Grilled Peaches (no more than one peach)
1 apple and ¼ cup raw nuts or seeds	Crowd-Pleasing Cioppino	Blueberry Cobbler (1 serving)
1 sliced tomato with avocado (about 2 tablespoons)	Chicken Marsala with Roasted Brussels Sprouts and a large green salad with 1 tablespoon balsamic vinaigrette	Magnificent Chocolate Macaroons (1 each)

WEEK 2 SUCCESS MENU

	BREAKFAST	SNACK	LUNCH
DAY 1	Totally Tofu Scramble	1 apple and 1 low-carb protein bar	Get Smart Mahi Mahi Burger (with low-carb, whole-grain bun or wrapped in romaine lettuce)
DAY 2	Tropical Storm Brain-Boosting Smoothie	2 cups chopped veggies with 2 tablespoons baba ghanouj	Avocado Wrap with added turkey
DAY 3	Brainy Breakfast Burrito (consider wrapping in romaine lettuce)	1 apple and ¼ cup raw nuts or seeds	Rainbow Quinoa Salad with added chicken breast
DAY 4	Sunrise Surprise Brain-Boosting Smoothie	2 cups raw veggies with ¼ cup guacamole	Peaceful Asian Pear Salad with added shrimp
DAY 5	Alpha Omega Oatmeal	Large green salad with tomatoes, 1 tablespoon olive oil and lemon juice and 1 tablespoon sunflower seeds	Low-Cal Lo Mein with Veggies with added shrimp
DAY 6	Chocolate-Covered Strawberry Brain-Boosting Smoothie	1 sliced tomato with sliced avocado (about 2 tablespoons)	Lemon Pepper Halibut with 1 head steamed broccoli
DAY 7	Gluten-Free Pancakes with Blueberries and Banana (1 small one) with 1 egg	2 cups veggies with 2 tablespoons hummus or Surprising Split Pea Hummus	Chicken Vegetable Wrap

WEEK 2 SUCCESS MENU

SNACK	DINNER	DESSERT
Green salad with 1 tablespoon olive oil and lemon juice	Pan Roasted Salmon with Vegetables	2 oz. Amazing Avocado Gelato
¼ cup raw nuts and seeds and ½ cup seeded grapes	Savory Lubian Rose Stew (brown rice optional, not suggested)	Warm Sweet Potato Pudding
Low-carb protein bar	Brain Fit Fajita Salad	½ cup Chocolate Mousse
Low-carb protein bar	Teriyaki Rice Bowl with Salmon	½ oz. extra dark chocolate (NOT MILK CHOCOLATE)
1 pear with ¼ cup raw nuts or seeds	Baked Salmon with Roasted Leeks	Grilled Peaches (1 each)
1 apple with ¼ cup raw nuts or seeds	Indian-Style Chicken with Creamy Broccoli Soup and green salad with 1 tablespoon vinaigrette dressing	Brain on Joy bar available at www.amenclinics.com
½ cup berries with ¼ cup raw nuts	Shirataki Noodles with Edamame and Smoked Salmon	Magnificent Chocolate Macaroons (1 each)

WEEK 1 SUCCESS MENU: VEGETARIAN

	BREAKFAST	SNACK	LUNCH
DAY 1	Berry Alert Brain-Boosting Smoothie	¼ cup raw almonds or sunflower seeds	White Bean Soup for the Wise
DAY 2	Feel-Good Eggs Ranchero	½ cup berries	Arugula Salad with Raspberries and Hemp Seeds with added tofu
DAY 3	Green Apple Goddess Brain Boosting Smoothie	¼ cup raw nuts or seeds	Very Veggie Pita
DAY 4	Guilt-Free Granola	Low-carb protein bar	Get Fit Fennel and Orange Salad with added tofu
DAY 5	Very Omega Cherry Brain-Boosting Smoothie	¼ cup nuts or seeds	Spinach and Strawberry Salad with Pecans with added tempeh
DAY 6	Coco Chunky Monkey Brain-Boosting Smoothie	Chopped veggies with Surprising Split Pea Hummus	Rainbow Quinoa Salad with seeds
DAY 7	Seafood Omelet for Super Focus with ¼ cup berries	¼ cup raw nuts or seeds	Stay Sharp Chard Salad with added tempeh

WEEK 1 SUCCESS MENU: VEGETARIAN

SNACK	DINNER	DESSERT
2 cups mixed veggies with 1 tablespoon hummus	Energizing Chipotle Enchiladas	2 oz. Amazing Avocado Gelato
Low-carb protein bar	Veggie Kabobs, Mung Bean Salad with 2 tablespoons mixed flax, hemp, and chia seeds	¼ cup Fruit Granita
1 crisp pear and 2 tablespoons raw nuts or seeds	"Spaghetti" and steamed broccoli	Brain on Joy bar available at www.amenclinics.com
½ cup berries of your choice and ¼ cup raw almonds	Tempeh with Vegetables	½ oz. extra dark chocolate (NOT MILK CHOCOLATE)
2 cups raw vegetables with 2 tablespoons guacamole	Barley Veggie Bowl with Sweet Potatoes with extra steamed veggies	Grilled Peaches (no more than one peach)
1 apple and ¼ cup raw nuts or seeds	Grilled Polenta with Roasted Beans	Blueberry Cobbler (1 serving)
1 sliced tomato with avocado (about 2 tablespoons)	Sinless Spinach Lasagna with Roasted Brussels Sprouts and a large green salad with 1 tablespoon balsamic vinaigrette	Magnificent Chocolate Macaroons (1 each)

WEEK 2 SUCCESS MENU: VEGETARIAN

	BREAKFAST	SNACK	LUNCH
DAY 1	Totally Tofu Scramble	1 apple and 1 low-carb protein bar	Portobello Burger (with low-carb, whole-grain bun)
DAY 2	Tropical Storm Brain-Boosting Smoothie	2 cups chopped veggies with 2 tablespoons baba ghanouj	Avocado Wrap with added tofu and seeds if desired, but there should be enough protein as is
DAY 3	Brainy Breakfast Burrito (consider wrapping in romaine lettuce)	1 apple and ¼ cup raw nuts or seeds	Rainbow Quinoa Salad with added tempeh
DAY 4	Sunrise Surprise Brain-Boosting Smoothie	2 cups raw veggies with ¼ cup guacamole	Grilled tofu and green salad with 1 tablespoon olive oil and lemon juice
DAY 5	Alpha Omega Oatmeal	2 cups veggies with 2 tablespoons hummus or Surprising Split Pea Hummus	Low-Cal Lo Mein with Veggies
DAY 6	Chocolate-Covered Strawberry Brain-Boosting Smoothie	1 sliced tomato with sliced avocado (about 2 tablespoons)	Keen Quinoa Pilaf with steamed broccoli
DAY 7	Gluten-Free Pancakes with Blueberries and Banana (1 small one) with 1 egg	Large green salad with tomatoes, 1 tablespoon olive oil and lemon juice and 1 tablespoon sunflower seeds	Lentil Pilaf

WEEK 2 SUCCESS MENU: VEGETARIAN

SNACK	DINNER	DESSERT
Green salad with 1 tablespoon olive oil and lemon juice	You'll Never Know It's Vegetarian Chili	2 oz. Amazing Avocado Gelato
¼ cup raw nuts and seeds and ½ cup seeded grapes	Vegetarian Savory Lubian Rose Stew	Peach Coconut Cream Dream
Low-carb protein bar	Brain Fit Fajita Salad with tempeh instead of chicken	½ cup Chocolate Mousse
Low-carb protein bar	Teriyaki Rice Bowl with tempeh instead of salmon	½ oz. extra dark chocolate (NOT MILK CHOCOLATE)
1 pear with ¼ cup raw nuts or seeds	Pasta Pomodoro and Easy Eggplant Parmesan with sautéed wax beans and baby bok choy	Grilled Peaches (1 each)
1 apple with ¼ cup raw nuts or seeds	Sinless Spinach Lasagna with Creamy Broccoli Soup and green salad	Brain on Joy bar available at www.amenclinics.com
1 cup berries with ¼ cup raw nuts	Shirataki Noodles with Edamame and tofu	Magnificent Chocolate Macaroons (1 each)

SHOPPING LIST
Chapter 12

SHOPPING LIST

Chapter 12

SHOPPING LIST

Shopping List

Vegetables:

asparagus

avocado

bell peppers, orange

bell peppers, red

bell peppers, yellow

bok choy

broccoli

Brussels sprouts

cabbage

carrots

celery

cucumber

endive

garlic

ginger

green beans

jalapeños

kale

leeks

lettuce, iceberg

lettuce, mixed greens

lettuce, romaine

mushrooms

mushrooms, portobello

mushrooms, shiitake

onions, green

onions, red

onions, white

onions, yellow

parsnips

potatoes, new

potatoes, russet

potatoes, white

radishes

scallions

shallots

snow peas

spinach leaves, baby

squash

squash, green

squash, spaghetti

squash, summer

squash, yellow

tomatoes

tomatoes, Roma

tomatoes, cherry or grape

yams or sweet potatoes

zucchini

Shopping List

Fruit:

apples, green

apples, red

bananas

blueberries

cantaloupe

cherries

coconut

grapefruit

grapes, green

grapes, red

lemon

lime

mango

oranges

papaya

peaches

pears

pineapple

raspberries

strawberries

Fresh Herbs:

basil

chives

cilantro

dill

marjoram

mint

oregano

parsley

rosemary

sage

thyme

Breads:

Ezekiel bread

Ezekiel pita bread

Ezekiel tortillas

gluten-free bread

multigrain bread (sugar-free)

sprouted-grain bread (sugar-free)

whole-wheat pita

whole-wheat tortillas (sugar-free)

Shopping List

Carton/Canned/Jarred Foods:

artichoke hearts

beans, black

beans, kidney

beans, pinto

capers

chicken broth, low-sodium (in a carton)

pasta sauce, organic

tomato paste

tomatoes, crushed

tomatoes, stewed

tomatoes, whole

tuna, albacore

vegetable broth, low-sodium (in a carton)

Packaged Foods:

bulgar wheat

cereal, organic

couscous

farro

grains

oats, old fashioned

oats, steel-cut

pearl barley

quinoa

rice, brown

Baking Aisle:

*Some of the oils may be found in the "specialty" section or may be purchased at a health food store.

almond oil

baking powder

baking soda

breadcrumbs, whole-wheat

coconut, raw and organic, no sugar added

coconut extract

coconut oil, refined

extra virgin olive oil

flour, oat

flour, rice

flour, soy

flour, spelt

flour, whole-wheat

honey, raw and unfiltered

maple extract

maple syrup, organic

sesame oil

vanilla extract

walnut oil

Shopping List

Nuts and Seeds:

almonds, raw

cashews, raw

chia seeds, raw

flax seeds, raw

pine nuts

pumpkin seeds, raw

sunflower seeds, raw

walnuts, raw

Pasta:

gluten-free pasta

risotto

spinach fettucini

whole-wheat fettucini

whole-wheat penne

whole-wheat spaghetti

Legumes:

black beans

garbanzo beans

kidney beans

lentils, green

lentils, red

lima beans

mung beans

pinto beans

split peas

Condiments:

balsamic vinegar

hoisin sauce

horseradish sauce

ketchup

mayonnaise, low-fat

mustard, Dijon

mustard, yellow

relish

salad dressing, light balsamic

salad dressing, other

salsa

soy sauce, low-sodium

teriyaki sauce

Worcestershire sauce

Shopping List

Spices and Seasonings:

allspice

basil

bay leaves

black pepper

cayenne pepper

chili powder

cinnamon, ground

cinnamon sticks

coriander, dried

cumin, ground

curry

ginger, ground

Himalayan pink salt

Italian seasoning

lemon pepper

nutmeg

oregano

paprika

Real Salt

red chili powder

red pepper flakes

sea salt

sesame seeds

thyme, dried

turmeric

white pepper

Refrigerator Case:

almond milk, unsweetened

Earth Balance®

eggs

egg substitute

rice milk

soy cream

soy milk

yogurt, low-fat and unsweetened (no artificial sweeteners)

Meat and Poultry:

*All meat should be organic free-range, organic, antibiotic-free, and hormone-free.

beef, Kobe

beef, Sirloin

chicken breast

chicken thighs

chicken, whole

ground turkey

turkey breast

turkey, whole

Seafood:

*Choose wild rather than farm-raised whenever possible; limit shellfish.

halibut, steaks or fillets

mackerel

mahi mahi

orange roughy

salmon, steaks or fillets

sardines

shrimp

snapper

swordfish

tuna, ahi

Freezer Case:

*Choose organic whenever possible.

blackberries

blueberries

broccoli

cherries

green beans

mixed vegetables

peas

raspberries

strawberries

Other:

baked chips, organic

cookies, sugar-free (no artificial sweeteners)

packaged soup mixes

taco seasoning

rice crackers

Shopping List

Specialty Items and Miscellaneous:

*These items will usually be found in the gourmet or health food section. Some may need to be purchased in a health food store.

arrowroot

cacao nibs, raw

cacao butter

cacao powder, raw

carob chips (use sparingly in recipes)

chia seeds

chlorella

coconut butter

coconut water

Earth Balance®

flax crackers (raw)

flax seed oil

flour, spelt

freeze dried greens powder

fruit-dried (eat sparingly)

goji berries

hemp seeds (no, they won't make you high)

honey, raw and unfiltered

maple syrup, organic

milk, almond

milk, coconut

milk, hemp

milk, rice

Parma! Vegan Parmesan® cheese by Eat In The Raw (this is a nut cheese and it is delicious!)

protein bars, low-sugar (use only in emergency)

protein powder, sugar-free (I prefer Vega® because it is loaded with nutrition and no sugar)

Shirataki noodles (I prefer the brand Miracle Noodles®)

spirulina

stevia

tamari sauce

tea, green

tea, herbal

Tofutti Better Than Cream Cheese® (use sparingly as it is a soy product, but I prefer it over dairy and it tastes great)

trail mix, raw and no added sugar, high fructose corn syrup, or sulfur dioxide

Vegenaise®, mayonnaise substitute

Most health food stores have a section dedicated to "raw foods" and "superfoods." This is my favorite section to shop in. I find the coolest snacks for my daughter's lunch there. But beware! These foods are not necessarily low-calorie! They are supercharged with phytonutrients, vitamins, and minerals and will give you a ton of energy, but you don't need to eat much. They are meant as a pick-me-up snack only! This is the section of the health food store that will get you seriously excited about eating healthy... BUT YOU STILL HAVE TO READ LABELS!

Acknowledgments

ACKNOWLEDGMENTS

I would first like to acknowledge my partner and cohort, Kamila Reschke. Your fabulous culinary skills, patience, and knowledge made this project possible. You are a true team player!

It is always with gratitude and love that I thank my husband, Daniel. Your willingness to be our guinea pig during the testing phase of the recipes is especially appreciated! You are an amazing life partner.

Special acknowledgment goes to Jaclyn Frattali for her amazing work on the book design and graphics.

I am eternally grateful to Frances Sharpe for her input and skill as a writer and editor.

Thanks and appreciation go to Catherine Miller and Breanne Payne for their attention to detail and dedication with gathering research.

Jim Kennedy, a wonderful photographer and artist, was a pleasure to work with.

To my precious daughter Chloe, who inspires me to keep my family and myself as healthy as possible. I love you with my whole heart!

ABOUT THE AUTHORS

Tana K. Amen, BSN

Tana Amen graduated magna cum laude from Loma Linda University with a Bachelor's of Science Degree in Nursing and has worked as a Trauma/Neurosurgical ICU nurse.

Tana is a health enthusiast and has been focused on fitness for over two decades. She also worked with some of the sickest patients in the hospital and saw the effects of poor lifestyle choices and the intense need for special nutrition when patients were healing from brain injuries and other traumas.

In spite of her medical and fitness background, Tana was repeatedly surprised when her own health failed her throughout the years. She was diagnosed with thyroid cancer at the age of 23. How could someone who lived a consciously healthy lifestyle be diagnosed with cancer and the numerous other health issues that presented themselves over the years? That's when she began to further her education about nutrition and the role it plays on overall health.

Tana began to realize that "health" and "fitness" are not synonymous. Furthermore, she came to the conclusion that many of the basic nutrition principles she had learned in her youth were outdated and not enough to optimize wellness in a person's life. There is a major difference between sustenance and optimal nutrition for a high-energy, passionately healthy lifestyle!

Tana is the nutrition and fitness leader of the Amen household. She practices martial arts regularly, has a black belt in Tae Kwon Do, and enjoys a variety of other physical activities. Keeping her family focused on fitness and health is a primary value for Tana.

ABOUT THE AUTHORS

Kamila Reschke

Kamila has more than 20 years of culinary expertise. She was born in Poland.

Influenced by her beloved grandmother's and later her mother's extraordinary cuisine, she followed their steps by attending different culinary schools in Poland.

She graduated from Technical School of Gastronomy in Tarnowskie Gory, Poland, with a Certified Chef in Technology and Cooking Techniques Degree/Certificate and later earned Bachelor's Degree in Art Sciences.

She moved to the United States of America in 1997 and has been developing her career by working as a personal gourmet chef for many people, including celebrities. Among them is a renowned psychiatrist, Dr. Amen, by whom she was encouraged to be the co-author of this book along with his wife.

Kamila is recognized and well-known for her amazing, healthy, kosher, and easy recipes and her creative, comprehensive abilities are far beyond imagination, borders, and culinary excellence.

She lives in Southern California with her husband and works for the Amen family.

ABOUT AMEN CLINICS, INC.

Amen Clinics, Inc. (ACI) specializes in helping people heal from behavioral, learning, emotional, cognitive and weight issues for children, teenagers, and adults. ACI has an international reputation for evaluating and treating:

- **Attention Deficit Disorder (ADD)**
- **Anxiety**
- **Depression**
- **School Failure**
- **Brain Trauma**
- **Obsessive Compulsive Disorders**

- **Bipolar Disorder**
- **Aggressiveness**
- **Marital Problems**
- **Substance Abuse**
- **Obesity**
- **Alzheimer's Disease and Memory Loss**

Brain SPECT imaging is one of the tools used by the Clinics. ACI has the world's largest database of brain SPECT scans related to behavioral problems. ACI welcomes referrals from physicians, psychologists, social workers, marriage and family therapists, drug and alcohol counselors, and individual clients.

Clinic Locations:

Southern California
4019 Westerly Place, Suite 100
Newport Beach, CA 92660

Pacific Northwest
616 120th Ave NE, Suite C100
Bellevue, WA 98005

Northern California
1000 Marina Blvd, Suite 100
Brisbane, CA 94005

East Coast
1875 Campus Commons Drive, Suite 101
Reston, VA 20191

Visit www.amenclinics.com or call 888-564-2700 for a consultation.

Amenclinics.com is an educational interactive brain website geared toward mental health and medical professionals, educators, students, and the general public. It contains a wealth of information to help you learn about our clinics and the brain. The site contains over 300 color brain SPECT images, thousands of scientific abstracts on brain SPECT imaging for psychiatry, a brain puzzle, and much, much more.

Visit Dr. Amen's new online solution that will hold your hand and give you all the tools you need to get thinner, smarter, and happier NOW, including:

- Detailed questionnaires to help you know your BRAIN TYPE and personalize this program to your own individual needs. You will also be able to test your memory and get a personalized plan to get thinner, smarter, happier, AND learn how to decrease your risk of Alzheimer's disease.

- There is an interactive daily online journal to track your important numbers, calories, and brain healthy habits, like sleep and exercise — THIS IS THE SINGLE MOST IMPORTANT TOOL FOR IMPROVING YOUR HEALTH.

- There are hundreds of brain healthy recipes, tips, shopping lists, and menu plans.

- Plus, you will get an exclusive, award-winning 24/7 BRAIN GYM MEMBERSHIP where you can test, work out and strengthen your brain to reduce stress, improve your memory and attention, and boost your mood. It is like having a personal trainer for YOUR OWN BRAIN. You will learn how your own brain works, train it specifically to fit your needs, and optimize your life. The brain gym has been described as "wildly fun...the positive thinking exercises have carried me through the day...."

- In addition, we will send you daily tips and even text messages to help you remember your supplements and stay on track to get healthy NOW.

- And whenever you feel sad, mad, nervous, or out of sorts, we will have exercises to help you boost your mood, decrease depression, and help you feel better fast.

- Plus much, much more.

- The online program is your personal guide to getting thinner, smarter, and happier.